SET YOUR HEART

A Pastor's Guide to Leading Sunday School Out of Exile

JUSTIN SMITH

ED&D BOOKS

DEDICATION

To Ken Coley, the teacher who inspired this work, walked with me through dark times, and continued to believe that this book could be written, even when its author was not always sure. May this serve as a tool for your toolbox as you continue to train God's people to do God's work around the world.

CONTENTS

Foreword by Allan Taylor   i

Acknowledgments   v

1   A Start To The Journey   1

2   The Basics   10

3   Leaders Must Be Found   24

4   Dealing With A Mess   36

5   Bring Out The Book   51

6   Getting Started   70

7   Final Thoughts   80

Appendix: Ezra's Leadership Behaviors   83
And Corresponding Behaviors For Pastors

References   85

About the Author   89

FOREWORD

The task of pastoring a local congregation is daunting! The pastor must be a wise theologian, shrewd financial expert, astute at building construction, masterful at organization, knowledgeable counselor, compassionate consoler, and a great family man! Whew, I'm weary just thinking about it! But of all the pastor is asked to do, leading his Sunday School must be a high priority. The problem is that seminary has prepared pastors for many things but seldom has equipped him to lead his Sunday School. Enter *Set Your Heart*.

The church has three great assets. They are not buildings, budgets, and location. These are assets indeed. They are valuable. They can be leveraged for the good of the church. They can aid the church in her mission. But they are not the church's greatest assets. The church in the book of Acts didn't possess any of the three. Yet, the church had power, influence, and transformed lives.

> "And the word of God increased, and the number of the disciples multiplied in Jerusalem greatly; and a great company of the priests were obedient to the faith." (Acts 6:7)

> "But the word of God grew and multiplied." (Acts 12:24)

> "So mightily grew the word of God and prevailed." (Acts 19:20)

What assets did the early church utilize? The same three assets we have at our deposal today – the Spirit of God, the word of God, and the people of God! We have the same Holy Spirit. We have the complete word of God whereas the New Testament was still being written in the early church era. And we have people – people born of God, a "chosen generation, a royal priesthood, a holy nation, a peculiar people" (1 Peter 2:9).

These three great church assets are powerful for they come from Almighty God! And these three great church assets have a meeting place – Sunday School! Jesus said that "where two or three are gathered together in my name, there am I in the midst of them" (Matthew 18:20). Sunday School binds the threefold cord of the Spirit of God, the word of God, and the people of God!

Therefore, Sunday School should be an effective and potent force in our churches for the Great Commission! So why are we not experiencing this? Sunday School is underutilized because it is underappreciated. When we underutilize our Sunday School we untie this threefold cord and essentially eliminate the church's third greatest asset – her people! We keep *having* Sunday School without *using* Sunday School. This means we are not leveraging our people with their Holy Spirit given giftedness for God's purpose and glory.

My friend, Justin Smith, has done a superb job in laying out steps every pastor can take to revitalize his Sunday School and maximize the threefold cord. You see, Sunday School must have leadership. Someone has to understand the value of Sunday School, have a God inspired vision for it, and then set plans of execution for its effectiveness. And no one can do that like the pastor!

Justin lays out simple and practical steps to help the always-busy pastor lead and equip his Sunday School. His *Four Stages of Group Development for Classes* provides the goal of every class and organizes training around them. Using the biblical example of Ezra, Justin offers three simple steps in recruiting workers, how to deal with sinful or unbiblical workers, how to establish guidelines for workers, and how to hold them accountable. *The Pastor's Sunday School Scorecard* is an outstanding tool for the pastor to employ. It will keep his leadership on track and move his Sunday School to greater effectiveness. Lastly, the *Leadership Behaviors* chart will serve to keep the big picture in mind as the key leader of your church's Sunday School.

Why should the pastor take such interest and leadership in Sunday School? Why should the pastor champion Sunday School?

Because the work of the Sunday School is the work of the church!

Pastor, your leadership matters...a lot! The value and importance of your leadership in your Sunday School is tantamount. Without it your Sunday School will most likely flounder. With it your Sunday School will most likely flourish! It is my prayer that you will read this book, embrace its teaching, and *Set Your Heart* on your Sunday School!

Allan Taylor
Director, Sunday School & Church Education Ministry
LifeWay Christian Resources
Nashville, TN

ACKNOWLEDGMENTS

Encouragement comes in many different forms; that was certainly the case for me when it came to writing this book! The idea for this book was conceived several years ago upon the completion of my doctoral dissertation and I am very thankful for the work of Dr. Ken Coley, Dr. Larry Purcell, and Dr. Tom Crites to help me complete and refine that research. But the actual birth of this work only became possible after several dear people provided encouragement at just the right time.

The challenge of my good friend, Dr. Micheal Pardue, to craft a book that could be used to help train pastors in the ins and outs of Sunday school as they lead the educational ministries of their churches was exactly the spark I needed to start this project in earnest. The remarkable Stephanie Miller fanned the flame again and again as she read over every chapter and encouraged me to keep working; this book owes much of its clarity to her encouragement! My coworkers at First Baptist Icard Child Enrichment Center served as prayer warriors and cheerleaders to finish the book, while my parents, Greg and Sue Smith, dared me to dream big and present a work that the church could use. My friend, Allan Taylor, generously provided the foreword and gave me a much-needed vote of confidence that the ideas I gave would be a help to Sunday schools and the churches they serve.

But I would be remiss if I did not acknowledge my biggest fans: my wonderful children! Nate, Joanna, and Sam have been true champions for me to carry out the work of writing this book! They have encouraged me to write, they have dreamed of seeing their names in my book, and they have served as my inspiration for completing a book of this nature. I want my children to experience a church where they study God's Word, care for one another, and share the gospel throughout the world as they worship our Lord Jesus Christ; it is for them and all who shall follow the Lord where He walks that I pray this book will bear fruit among pastors who

v

seek to lead their Sunday school.

1

A START TO THE JOURNEY

Sunday School.

In a pastor's world, there are few words that bring as wide of an array of emotions as these two. For some, it is the enigma that cannot be solved; for others, it is the dead horse that people keep trying to ride. Sunday school is one of the few mainstays that has weathered decades of change in the way that churches are conducted, yet for many pastors, it has become something to stand off from and let others deal with, with the hope that it does not come back to bite the pastor unexpectantly.

But the intent of Sunday school was not to become an albatross around the church's neck that pastors would have to wrestle with; no, it had a much higher calling from the start. David Francis (2011), in his short history work, *Missionary Sunday School*, gives a great overview of the history of Sunday school, noting that Sunday school began as a missionary movement apart from the church with the goal of reaching, teaching, and ministering to persons who were outside the church and far from God. It would be shocking to many in our time to know that Sunday school attendance far outpaced worship service attendance for much of America's existence.

While it may not always present itself as such, research continues to indicate that Sunday school is still one of the most effective ministries in growing churches today. Rainer (1999) concluded in his study of effective evangelistic churches that "The research is clear if not overwhelming. Sunday school is *the* most effective assimilation methodology in evangelistic churches today" (p.36). In their more recent study on comeback churches that turned from a declining state to a state of growth, Stetzer and Dodson (2010) found Sunday school to be one of the top ten factors for church revitalization, leading them to call the ministry the "Velcro that holds the revitalization process together" (p.197). Stetzer and Rainer (2010) found that transformational churches emphasized Sunday school at a significantly higher rate than other churches, noting that it became the primary means to connect members into smaller communities that could bring about life change.

But I know what you are thinking: "That's great and all, but how does knowing that Sunday school was supposed to be about reaching, teaching, and ministering help me now?" Or even more, "just because Sunday school has been effective for fast growing churches or revitalizing churches or even transformational churches, how can it help me?"

Sunday School Can Help, But…

When Sunday school is functioning well, it is one of the most powerful vehicles a church has to help it carry out the Great Commission and to engage members in doing Christ's work. While many churches have moved away from the name "Sunday school," the heart of the ministry remains the same: it is a group that is open, ongoing, and employs a plan to study the Bible. Gene Mims (2003) describes these open groups as person-centered (meaning they focus on bringing people into a transforming relationship with God), lay-led, and Bible-based, concluding that open groups fulfill the Great Commission by making disciples of all men. Though they are often called classes because of the Sunday school name, Mims called this a misnomer, explaining, "They are classes in the sense that the Bible is studied, but they are much more. They are kingdom entities built on the five functions of the church. They are living organisms built for the people who attend" (p.135).

But this sounds nothing like what most pastors hear from the Sunday school or small groups that take place in their churches. Any pastor would get behind a strategy that would help him assimilate newcomers into a group of believers, study the Scriptures each week, connect believers together to care for one another, and mobilize believers to share their faith and take the gospel throughout the world. Sunday school was designed to be that strategy, but in our day, it has fallen into disrepair. In many churches today, Sunday school sits like an old rusty car, shining in places with a bit of its past glory, but by and large is no more than a lawn ornament. To make matters worse, pastors are often given the keys to this car with no instructions on how to start it, how to make it run, or even how to drive it. The goal of this book is to give you, as a pastor and leader, an owner's manual of sorts to help you dust off the wear and tear of Sunday school in your church and prepare you to not only get it started again, but to hear it hum and purr again as a vehicle to carry Christ's disciples in their Great Commission work.

One of the struggles for pastors is that there are simply not many resources available today to guide a pastor in leading Sunday school. While the market is filled with works on how to lead an individual group or on the importance of groups, little attention has been given to practical steps that pastors can take to help Sunday school in their churches. But this is not the market's fault, but rather, a reflection of the emphasis given to Sunday school; it is often neglected in seminaries and Bible colleges tasked with training pastors and is rarely used in churches as beginning training for prospective pastors. Steve Parr (2010) laments over his experience of talking with a large group of master of divinity graduates, those who have been trained for the task of pastoring, who had been given no academic training at all concerning how to lead Sunday school, leading him to conclude, "if the pastor does not have the tools and the knowledge, neither will the members. The result is that many pastors go into a church that has the basic Sunday school structure… but the Sunday school is lifeless and cold" (p.21).

Further, with the many other tasks that occupy a pastor's schedule and thinking, Sunday school is often placed on the back burner. In trying to understand why pastors were not more involved in Sunday school, Rainer (1999) found that pastors focused their attentions on the corporate worship service, allowing Sunday school to become a secondary concern and run itself. Taylor (2009) argued that many pastors were overly infatuated with the worship service and preaching, noting that "My point here is not to minimize worship and preaching. My goal is to strike a balance in the way a pastor leads the church" (p.3). But I would like to propose that part of the reason this has become the case among pastors is simply that they are not equipped and able to understand what role they should play in Sunday school. Indeed, the tyranny of the urgent and the fear of not being able to lead competently often leads pastors to stand on the sidelines, missing the great joy and responsibility that can be seen in Sunday school. As Taylor (2009) reminds us, Sunday school is important because it "handle[s] the two most precious things to God every week – God's Word and God's people. I do not know of anything God loves more than His Word and His people" (p.56).

Hope From An Unexpected Source

But let's be honest for a moment; Sunday school may be a great tool, but is there any way that we can turn it around at this point to make it useful in today's day? Have we gone too far to be able to fix it? Lest we should lose hope, we do have a model in the Old Testament that can both encourage and inspire us: Ezra the Scribe.

Now to be fair, Ezra seems like an unlikely choice as one who could inspire and guide pastors in their work; after all, he was never a pastor himself. For that matter, he really does not appear as a major character in the scope of Old Testament history. He is only mentioned in five chapters of the Scriptures and even the book that bears his name only follows him for four out of ten chapters. Even in the passages that name him, Ezra often serves as a part of the supporting cast, often emerging from the side of the stage or the room of the house rather than taking center stage. How can he be an example for pastors in how to lead Sunday school?

The beauty of Ezra's example comes not in how impressive his credentials were, though as a member of priestly lineage and a scribe of the highest regard they were certainly impressive, but his example serves us well for two significant reasons: his task and his commitment. Following seventy years of Judah's exile in Babylon, the Lord, through a series of political maneuverings among the nations, allowed His people to return to the Promised Land under the Persians' rule. With the remarkable support of King Artaxerxes, Ezra was sent to Jerusalem and outfitted with anything he requested (Ezra 7:6). As part of his plan to stabilize Judah and the southern part of his kingdom, Artaxerxes' commission to Ezra is found in Ezra 7:12-26, where the scribe was given two major directives: determine whether the people are living according to the law of God and restore them to a rightful worship of God according to that law. To this end, Artaxerxes both directed and empowered Ezra in Ezra 7:25 to judge and teach the people according to the Law of God; miraculously, the pagan king was concerned that all of the Jews be under the same law – God's law. In short, Ezra was commissioned to lead the people back to the Scriptures by assessing their current adherence to God's law, instructing them where they lacked in their knowledge of the law, and correcting them when they disobeyed it so that they may properly worship God in His temple.

While pastors and leaders are not often given the government's approval and endorsement to lead God's people back into a study and application of His Word to their lives, we are no less called to lead God's people into a study of his Word so that they may worship the Lord according to His ways. In considering how pastors may lead Sunday school in their churches, we are facing a situation similar to Ezra's: pastors are commissioned with assessing the lives of those in their churches and instructing them in God's Word, correcting them where they err, and encouraging them where they lack. In this way, Ezra serves as an exemplar model for us, for in seeing how he led the people of Israel back into the Scriptures and into right worship of the Lord, we can learn behaviors that we can use today as we seek to guide and shepherd the Sunday school and small groups in our church who exist to teach God's Word and help her people to live that Word out, both in ministry to one another and in taking the gospel throughout the world.

The Layout of this Book

The layout of this book is designed to help you start from the beginning of assessing and directing your Sunday school or small groups. Chapter two will begin with a look at the strategy behind Sunday school and a simple guide to help you assess your groups and program as a whole. In chapters three, four, and five, we will walk with Ezra through his leadership of the Jewish people in Ezra 7-10 and Nehemiah 8, gleaning principles from the leadership behaviors he demonstrates and applying them to how you can lead in today's church. Chapter six will bring together the principles we have learned and give you a plan to begin implementing these leadership behaviors into your ministry. As we journey through these concepts, each chapter will end with questions for discussion, designed to help you probe through the material of the chapter, as well as a chance for deeper thought, which are assignments to help you dig deeper into the material.

Throughout this book, I will use the term Sunday school, but there are certainly other labels that your church may use, including Bible study groups, Bible Fellowship, Life Groups, Life Application Groups, Small Groups, Home Teams, or even simply Groups. The name is not so much the vital part as much as the mission or goal of these groups. Sunday school expert Josh Hunt (1997) describes Sunday school as a strategy used to organize a congregation into smaller groups for the purpose of "teaching, caring, sharing, reaching, loving, encouraging, and helping" (p.9). David Francis (2011) clarified that "A group that is open, ongoing, and employs a systematic Bible study plan is functionally equivalent to a Sunday school class, whatever you call it" (p.27). In that spirit, whenever you see the word Sunday school, feel free to use your functionally equivalent name; the goal is learning how to lead, not taking on a new label.

A Necessary Consideration

Before we close this chapter, though, I would be remiss if I did not mention the part of Ezra's witness that should inspire us most: his character. Ezra 7:10 records that "Ezra had set his heart to study the Law of the Lord, and to do it and to teach his statutes and rules in Israel" (ESV). Certainly Ezra's priestly heritage and scribal ability uniquely qualified him to help lead Israel to restore a true worship of God in the midst of a Persian occupation, but to assume that his skills and ability alone allowed him to succeed in his reformation work would overlook the importance of Ezra's character and would overlook the importance that our character will play as we lead. Ezra was not merely a leader or a student, but rather, a practitioner of the Law and a teacher of its ways. The threefold commitment to studying, practicing, and teaching the Scriptures built into Ezra's character a strong reliance on God and allowed him to powerfully lead a nation struggling with its spiritual identity upon the return from the exile. The Law was not a dead letter for Ezra, but rather, a call to action to follow the Lord that he could pour his heart into and walk in. Derek Kidner (1979) masterfully summarized the importance of this verse in understanding Ezra's lasting influence:

> He is a model reformer in that what he taught he had first lived, and what he lived he had first made sure of in the Scriptures. With study, conduct and teaching put deliberately in this right order, each of these was able to function properly at its best: study was saved from unreality, conduct from uncertainty, and teaching from insincerity and shallowness. (p.62)

Before you consider anything else regarding Sunday school or church ministry in general, you must come to grips with this reality: are you willing to set your heart to studying the Word so that you may know the Lord? Are you willing to obey God? Are you willing to pour out to others what God has poured into you through His Word? You can have the best strategy in the world and the greatest leaders among men, but if you are not willing to set your heart upon the ways of the Lord and follow Him, it will all be a waste. On the other hand, if you are willing to set your heart to study God's Word for yourself, obey it, and teach it to others, you may very well see your Sunday school come out of Exile.

Questions for Discussion

1. How would you describe the state of Sunday school at your church? Are you happy with it?
2. Why do you think pastors struggle to lead Sunday school?
3. What do you hope to gain from reading this book?

A Chance for Deeper Thought

The chapter concludes with a call to set your heart to study God's Word, apply it in your life, and teach it to others. Imagine that a new pastor has written to you asking how he could improve

Sunday school at his church. In a 2-3 page letter to this pastor, explain why he must begin by setting his heart on Bible study, application, and teaching to see revival in his Sunday school and church. Please use Scripture and personal experiences to help our pastor friend understand!

2

THE BASICS

Every skill starts with the basics. An artist must learn to sketch before she can paint a masterpiece. A carpenter must learn to hammer a nail before he can frame a house. In understanding the basics of a thing, one can grasp the strategy and the skills it will take to perfect it.

Years back, I had the privilege of serving in a sports ministry in Charlotte, NC; while I was there, we had the opportunity to partner with the then-Charlotte Bobcats to have a special Sunday afternoon game for our ministry. As part of this promotion, I was sent to the arena several hours before the game to coordinate all of the giveaways and audience participation games with the Bobcats staffers. After we had gotten all of our ducks in a row, it came time for the opposing team, the Toronto Raptors, to warm up with their shootaround. I noticed that one of their players, Kyle Lowry, who was merely a high draft pick and backup point guard at the time, spent the entire thirty minutes dribbling up and down the midcourt line. He would take a few trips dribbling with his right hand, then a few with his left; he would take several trips dribbling between his legs, then several more behind his back as he ran. At first, this seemed like such a waste of time to me; after all, this was a professional basketball player, surely dribbling should be like second nature to him. But as I continued to watch, I began to respect the brilliance in his approach; he was mastering the art of dribbling, which was the tool of his craft, even in the little moments that no one else saw. It should come as no shock that Kyle Lowry has repeatedly been honored as an All-Star in the NBA!

The people who really know their craft begin by clearly understanding what they are trying to accomplish and which tools are at their disposal for their task. Unfortunately, when it comes to Sunday school, leaders are often unclear as to the goal or purpose they are aiming for. In an era where associational or state leadership rarely has the opportunity to host or provide Sunday school training en masse to its churches and seminaries rarely lead students to understand the fundamentals of Sunday school, churches and their pastors are simply no longer equipped with a basic grasp of what Sunday school is trying to accomplish or how it does this. In this chapter, the goal is to provide just that: a basic grasp of the goal of Sunday school and a systemic overview to understand how Sunday school can grow one class at a time.

The Goal of Sunday School

In one of the best Sunday school books of our day, *Sunday School in HD*, Allan Taylor (2009) explains, "We have correctly been taught that Christians ought to do what Jesus did. I submit to you that Sunday school should also do what Jesus did!" (p.34). But what did Jesus do when it came to public ministry?

The Gospel of Matthew offers of us two looks into the public ministry of Jesus that are strikingly parallel. The first is found in Matthew 4:23:

And he went throughout all Galilee, teaching in their

> synagogues and proclaiming the gospel of the kingdom
> and healing every disease and every affliction among the
> people.

The second is found just five chapters later in Matthew 9:35:

> And Jesus went throughout all the cities and villages,
> teaching in their synagogues and proclaiming the gospel
> of the kingdom and healing every disease and every
> affliction.

Following Jesus' ministry through the cities of Israel reveals three common activities that Jesus engaged in that inform what we should be doing with Sunday school. First, Jesus went into the synagogues to teach. The synagogue would have been the place where the Scriptures could be found and where people came to learn about the Lord. His work was marked by a devotion to teach God's Word to His people, a mark that should also serve as a first priority for our ministry today.

But Jesus' work did not end in the synagogue, but rather, went into all the city, as Jesus proclaimed the gospel of the kingdom. The Greek term used here is *kerusso*, which carries the force of announcing something aloud or proclaiming it aloud. The idea is that Jesus is acting as a herald, an announcer of sorts, proclaiming to all the good news that the kingdom is near. We often use a similar term to describe this: evangelism! In evangelism, we are proclaiming the good news that the kingdom is near and that Christ has given us entry into it through his death and resurrection. We are calling those who live in the domain of darkness to repent of their sins and be transferred into the kingdom of Christ Jesus, in whom we have redemption, the forgiveness of sins (Col. 1:13).

There was a third activity, though, that was constant in Jesus' public ministry: He healed every disease and affliction. Notice how Matthew does not put a limit on the types of therapy our Lord gave, allowing it to cover every disease and affliction, literally anything that makes a person soft. It is remarkable that Jesus was not merely content with teaching truth or proclaiming the kingdom, but rather, He laid an emphasis on ministering to those who were heavy laden. We carry on the same heart when we care for those in our midst who are hurting and suffering.

When we put these three actions together, we begin to get a clear picture of the goal of Sunday school based on Jesus' ministry. Jesus dedicated His time to teaching the Word of God, proclaiming the coming kingdom, and healing those who suffered. In the same way, our Sunday school should reflect these three values as well: we should be teaching people, reaching people, and ministering to people (Taylor, 2009).

At first glance, it may seem too simple to state that the aim of Sunday school should be teaching people, reaching people, and ministering to people. Yet, the structure of committing open, small groups to carrying out these aims is what sets Sunday school apart from many ministries dedicated to one or two of these aims alone. For instance, one of the strengths of Sunday school is that it utilizes a small group environment where all three of these goals can be pursued. Carrying out the task of ministering to an entire church would be daunting, even in a smaller body, but breaking the body down into smaller groups allows the class to minister to those within their group, making the work much more manageable and multiplying the number of people involved in ministering to the hurting.

Further, simply having several groups provides another opportunity for the church to equip and send leaders into the work of the kingdom. If each group is to meet the goals of teaching, reaching, and ministering to people, then each group will need leaders to guide those functions, giving the church the chance to train and equip more of its members and giving them a place to serve. In other words, Sunday school not only gives members a place to be involved and a place to belong, but it also serves as a training ground for future leaders to learn and practice the three goals of Sunday school. Both through groups reproducing and new believers responding to the gospel proclaimed by the groups,

Sunday school can provide a church with an ever-growing vehicle to assimilate new believers, train and equip them in God's Word, and involve them in proclaiming the gospel and caring for one another.

But just knowing what the target looks like does not ensure that we are actually shooting at it, much less hitting the bullseye. After all, many failed endeavors had wonderful mission statements guiding their values, but the missing ingredient in the graveyard of great ideas was often not the foundational values, but rather, the systems needed to help leaders assess their current position and give direction to which way they should move.

A System to Guide Sunday School Toward Growth

Not too long ago, I found that my dishwasher had sprung a leak! Now when I took off the faceplate to my dishwasher, at first glance, it just looked like a jumbled mess of plastic and metal parts covered in water. I knew the general purpose of the appliance, but at the moment, that did not help the situation; I needed a picture from the top-down of how this machine worked so I could see where the water would be coming from and how to address the problem. With a little help from a search engine, I was able to find the schematic drawings of the dishwasher and track down the part that was broken; what began as confusion and flooding ended with a simple replacement of a water valve.

Unfortunately, most pastors have not been given a schematic to know how the Sunday school should work or what the process for growth and development should be. In many ways, they are asked to be a repairman for an appliance that they have never seen working well or never had explained to them before. I would like to propose, though, that understanding Sunday school strategy can be as simple as thinking about how a family matures.

Consider how a family moves through various stages as children grow. With younger children, parents are not aiming to be friends or buddies, but rather, are called upon to be teachers and guides. Family life begins by teaching children the values of the family and helping them to know the difference in right and wrong. In the same way, Sunday school begins in the teaching phase, where the goal is to understand what God is saying in His Word and learning how to apply it and live by it. By beginning with learning and applying God's Word, we are helping our students understand the values of the Kingdom and know how they handle life and live it as God has called them.

But eventually, children grow out of their elementary stages of life and grow into the dreaded teenage years. Part of the reason that teenagers appear to be hard to get along with is that they are in the midst of a major transition; they are no longer children, yet they are also not mature enough to be independent adults. So, in this stage, they are testing out their boundaries, stretching their legs a bit to try to run, and looking back home to see if their parents will still help them and take care of them if they fall. Likewise, once students have begun to learn the truths of Scripture in Sunday school, they will begin to test whether those values are true and whether the promises of God really hold up. It is during this stage that students need to know they have someone that cares about them and will help them up if they fall. In this caring stage of Sunday school, groups are not merely functioning as classes, but they are beginning to become families that pray for each other, take care of one another, and spend time together.

Those teenagers will become human again, though, and grow into young adults. This is an exciting, but scary time of life for the family, as the family begins to grow with boyfriends and girlfriends who eventually turn into spouses. Not only is the family growing, but the children are preparing to take flight into the world, setting out on new careers and leaving the nest to carry the values of the family out into the world. We might call this the going stage for our Sunday school analogy, as it is this stage where our groups that have become like family take the Kingdom values out into the world. Having learned the truths of the gospel and having a group of believers supporting and caring for them, students in this stage are ready to take the gospel out into the world by inviting others into the group and finding ways to work together in missions and in ministry.

Finally, there comes the point in every family where the baby bird begins a family of her own. It eventually becomes time for the children to start a home of their own with their spouses and a whole new family unit begins. Sunday school also replicates family life in this stage as well, as healthy groups will reproduce after their own kind, sending out people to form new groups. The goal of Sunday school has never been to produce mammoth classes, but rather, it has always been to continue reproducing new small groups, giving more and more people the chance to get involved and carry out the work of the Kingdom. Just as parents take joy in seeing their children having children of their own, Sunday school groups experience great joy in seeing their investment in God's Word and one another bring fruit in beginning new groups who will teach God's Word, care for one another, and go to make disciples.

These four stages of group development, then, give us a simple system that we can use in a variety of ways to help us assess and direct Sunday school at various stages of the organization. Below, you will see a diagram that has been adapted from Taylor's (2009) Cycle of Teacher Maturation, showing the flow of Sunday school development, beginning at the top with Teach and rotating clockwise until it reaches Send and starts over again.

The Four Stages of Group Development

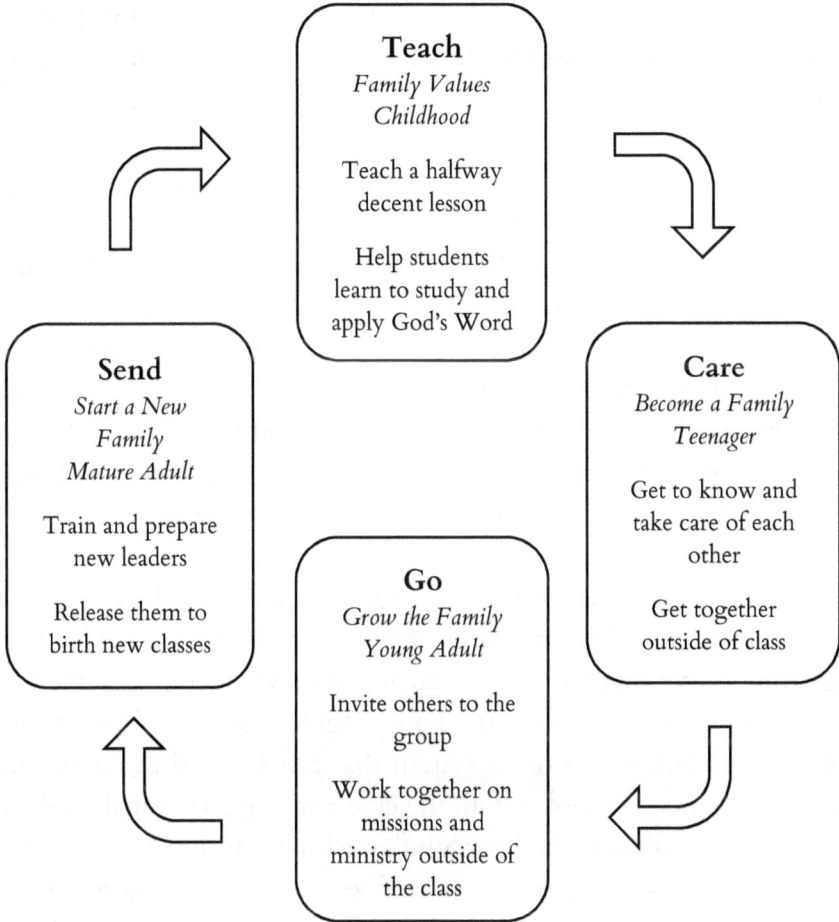

Teach
Family Values
Childhood

Teach a halfway
decent lesson

Help students
learn to study and
apply God's Word

Send
*Start a New
Family*
Mature Adult

Train and prepare
new leaders

Release them to
birth new classes

Go
Grow the Family
Young Adult

Invite others to the
group

Work together on
missions and
ministry outside of
the class

Care
Become a Family
Teenager

Get to know and
take care of each
other

Get together
outside of class

One of the unique parts of leading Sunday school comes from the reality that you are leading an organization of organizations; you are leading on two planes concurrently, as you are responsible both for the organization as a whole in your church, as well as the individual classes themselves. It is this two plane nature that makes leading Sunday school difficult because most leaders' tendency is to emphasize one plane and ignore the other. Many pastors, for instance, tend to emphasize organizational themes or goals in Sunday school, but are often uninvolved at the class level, resulting in a number of vision statements or campaigns that are launched from the church office, but never land in the class rooms. Further, a lack of involvement on the class level leaves many pastors vulnerable, as they are unable to get a grasp on the teaching or effectiveness of individual groups and can be easily blindsided by actions from a particular group or leader that have gone unchecked.

On the other hand, many Sunday school leaders can become hyper focused on the class level to the neglect of organizational leadership. Sunday school leadership is often made up of those who have succeeded as teachers, so it very natural for them to focus in on what they know: the week to week mechanics of running an individual group. However, without a cohesive organizational leadership, there is no way to build unity and consistency among the various groups within a church, often resulting in a few classes with gifted leaders thriving, while several others struggle to continue.

The effective pastor leading Sunday school must lead on both planes concurrently, not settling to merely make broad themes, nor getting overly involved in particular classes while letting some rot on the vine. The benefit of the Four Stages of Group Development strategy is that it lays out a system that can be used to assess and evaluate Sunday school at both the class and organizational level, as well as give guidance for how Sunday school can continue to grow on both planes. To help you maximize the value of this system, I want to walk you through how to use this tool, first at the class level and then organizationally.

The Four Stages of Group Development for Classes

One of the struggles pastors often experience is knowing where to start when it comes to getting involved with Sunday school. While this book will cover a number of leadership behaviors that pastors may use to engage and lead Sunday school, a great place to start is to use the four stages of group development as a way to quickly assess and evaluate individual groups and begin to give direction on how the group can continue to grow.

The first place we begin is in the Teach stage, where we are concerned with the teaching of Word of God. The first goal that we have in Sunday school is that people are exposed to God's Word and can learn how to study and apply it for themselves. If we have accomplished nothing else in our small groups, we want the students to walk away having learned something of who God is, what He is telling us to do, and how we can do it; this can only come through a study of God's Word and continued training on how to apply the truths of Scripture to our lives. So, then, the starting point for evaluating classes is to determine, "Do people learn to study and apply God's Word in this class?"

The call for teaching is not to produce a new commentary of the Bible week after week, but rather, it is expose people to God's Word and challenge them to learn from it and follow it. To this end, Josh Hunt (1997) has championed the concept of teaching a "halfway decent lesson," meaning that the aim of the lesson is to engage every student in the Scriptures, even if that means that the delivery method is not picture perfect. At the baseline, the hope is that every person has the opportunity to hear and learn from the Scriptures; if this is the case, then the class is prepared to move to the next stage. If this is not the case, though, then the action plan is clear – work with the class leaders concerning how to teach a halfway decent lesson.

Continuing clockwise through our diagram, we can see that the second stage of group development, Care, is concerned with how we care for one another within the group. There are two components to this stage, as we both want our groups to know each other and to care for each other. While our Bible teaching may be on point, if our group does not know and like each other, it will be hard for them to actually take care of one another. One of the starting points for the Care stage, then, considers how does the group get to know one another personally? Does the group have a way to welcome newcomers into the fold? Are they making plans to get to know each other better through things like parties or social gatherings? Is it evident in class that the members of the group actually know one another well?

The reason it is critical to know one another is that the next step of the Care stage comes in ministry within the group. That is, the members of the group must know each other well enough to learn each other's needs and be able to help meet those needs and serve one another. As you survey the class, you can begin to see if there is a clear way that members of the group pray for one another or care for one another in times of crisis, like a surgery or death in the family. Caring for one another at a class level is rarely spontaneous; it takes organization and a leader to coordinate things like making phone calls to members who have been absent or setting up visits for an ailing group member. When it seems that the group knows one another and genuinely has planned to take care of one another, the group is ready to move to the third stage of group development.

The third stage, Go, is often the most neglected stage in the development of a group. Teaching is normally seen as the goal of Sunday school and, with a little encouragement, groups often enjoy caring for one another, but the idea of taking the gospel out into the world is often a frightful event for many. Further, as the group has grown more and more into a family, members sometimes become hesitant to invite others into the group, preferring to stay close to their friends. Nonetheless, the natural development of groups calls for the group to expand their circles and to take the gospel out to reach the lost. The Go stage has two major emphases, as groups work to bring in and go out.

The first emphasis point involves inviting others to join the group and sharing the gospel personally to others. The mere presence of visitors is often a good sign that a group has not become closed and is bringing others into the class. Further, a class emphasis on being able to share the gospel and share one's testimony of how they came to Christ can equip members to be prepared and motivated to share the gospel with the lost. But the Go stage also includes preparing to go out; the goal is for the group to meet at other times in the week for the purpose of serving others and sharing the gospel. Projects of this nature require coordination and a leader is often chosen among the class to lead the missions or evangelism efforts of the group.

Finally, if a group has worked to teach a halfway decent lesson each week, get to know and care for one another, and invite others and take the gospel into the world, they are prepared to move into the final stage of group development, the Send stage, where they prepare leaders to become teachers, care leaders, and go leaders for new classes. There is no magic number as to how big of a class is too big or when a new class needs to form, but a general rule of thumb is that a class is prepared to birth a new class when it is too large to care for itself. In general, a person can care for about three families well, so when the class has grown larger than its leadership base can care for, it is a good sign that a new class is ready to be birthed. However, this is not a task that takes place overnight, as leaders need to be trained and prepared. The effective group that reaches the Send stage is preparing for the future by enlisting apprentices at the three key leader positions of teacher (Teach), shepherd (Care), and guide (Go) to both train them and give them opportunities to practice and grow. Once a new group begins, the process restarts, asking if the groups continue to Teach and moving through the stages.

As you can see through this walk-through, having a simple, clear strategy for Sunday school gives you a way to assess on the class level where a group is in its development and gives the group direction as to which skills it needs to work toward to continue to grow.

The Four Stages of Group Development for the Organization

While the Four Stages of Group Development can guide a group to develop and grow, the question becomes: how does this help me in the organizational level? Looking at Sunday school from the top-down, the four stages become the core values of the organization that serve as the basis for training and developing quality standards. Since the same values are used as the scorecard for all classes, training can become standardized and focused; rather than struggling to train all facets of Sunday school in sporadic training meetings, the pastor can focus on one stage at a time, beginning by training his teachers in teaching a bible lesson and moving from there. The strength of having a common language and process as the basis of the strategy is that the leader has a direction in training and can continually refer to the core values in working with class leaders.

Unity of values on the organizational level becomes a huge momentum builder for the pastor, as he can unite the Sunday school with the church's mission statement; Sunday school can become an extension of his ministry, rather than an obstacle, and can reinforce the goals of teaching God's word, caring for one another, and going to make disciples. Even more, the consistency from the organization to the class allows the pastor's words to resonate more clearly at the class level as you begin to speak the same organizational language, for the same values taught in the worship service are seen in the Sunday school.

One note should be considered at this point, though, concerning the labels used in the Four Stages of Group Development. One of the strengths of systems thinking is that the labels are not necessarily as important as the function in the systems. In this case, I used the labels Teach, Care, Go, and Send because those labels fit the concepts simply and clearly, but you are welcome to attach the verbiage used in your mission or vision statement to the process as well. These four stages have worked in a variety of contexts and have taken on names like Reach Up, Reach In, Reach Out, and Reach On. Either way, the concepts are still the same, so use the labels that resonate with your church's vision most clearly; the goal is not to reinvent Sunday school, but rather, it is to clarify the goal and organize the actions of Sunday school.

With a simple strategy to guide your approach to Sunday school, the wise pastor can quickly assess the condition of his Sunday school and know where he can begin to work with his leaders to help them carry out the task of teaching God's Word, proclaiming the gospel of the Kingdom, and caring for those who are hurting and in need. Knowing the basics of Sunday school should give you a good starting point to begin considering what we can learn from Ezra the scribe as we seek to guide our people back into the Word of God.

Questions for Discussion

1. What are the some of the goals you have for Sunday school at your church?
2. Do you think it would help pastors to have a strategy for Sunday school? Why or why not?
3. How would knowing the Four Stages of Group Development help a pastor to lead on a class level?
4. What are some benefits of having a clear, simple strategy for Sunday school on the organizational level?

A Chance for Deeper Thought

One of the key concepts of this chapter is understanding the Four Stages of Group Development. These stages are based on model of Jesus' ministry in Matthew and are demonstrated throughout Scripture as the role of believers in the church. To help you further consider these stages, choose one of the four stages and, in a 2-3 page essay, give a biblical justification for why a church should hold that stage as a core value.

3

LEADERS MUST BE FOUND

Considering the simple strategy for Sunday school laid out in chapter two, it becomes clear that leaders are vital to the success of Sunday school. Francis and Braddy (2013) detail well the need for every group to have at least three leaders: a teacher that stands before the group, a shepherd that sits among the group and cares for it, and a leader to take the group out into the world with the message of the Kingdom. But for the pastor who is already struggling to make sense of Sunday school, the thought of having to recruit, much less train, not only one leader, but three leaders may lead many to give up from the start. Despite our wishes to the contrary, leaders do not spontaneously arrive in positions of authority, nor are they usually prepared and equipped for the task ahead of them. Leaders must be found and developed.

A Look at How Ezra Recruited and Trained Leaders

Yet, modern day pastors are not alone in this need to both

recruit leaders with potential and develop them for service. In fact, Ezra's story begins in the same place as many pastors' today; he has a calling to restore the proper worship of God in Israel, but he does not have the leaders for the task. As the journey from Babylon to Jerusalem began in Ezra 8, the scribe and the families who agreed to return to Israel, a band made up of priests and laymen traveling with their families, gathered at a river just outside of Babylon to prepare for the trip that awaited them. It was during this time that Ezra made his first inspections of his traveling party, but as he did, he discovered a fatal flaw with his group: he had no Levites.

The Levites, descendants from the smallest tribe of Levi in Israel, were set apart by God to service the tabernacle during Israel's exodus in the wilderness. Upon the completion of Solomon's temple, the Levites' role as the barrier between the priests and the congregation expanded to that of the overseers of the house of the Lord. They were choristers, musicians, gatekeepers, judges, craftsmen, supervisors of the chambers and courts, and overseers of the temple treasury and royal officers. The Levites alone were explicitly permitted to approach the sacred furniture of the temple, giving them the honor and responsibility to serve God in a sacred position that was quite distinct from the rest of the community (McCready, 1986). Thus, the Levites were the skilled artists and managers who led the people to worship God and allowed the priests to offer sacrifices on their behalf. In calling people back to God's word and the true worship of God, then, it would be essential to have these servants of the temple in place. Yet, Kidner (1979) argued that the absence of the Levites and other temple servants is a revealing contretemps, as the Levites would not only be forced to leave the comfort of their newfound home in Babylon, but would have to leave the freedom of ordinary pursuits for the rigor and strictness of the Temple services. Myers (1965) continued that the neglect of this group during the Exile led them to use their considerable talents to engage in other work, making Ezra's call to return to a life of servanthood in Israel an even taller task.

Recruiting is never an easy task, especially when the position may not be the most exciting of places to serve, but Ezra's strategy to secure the Levites he needed to be a part of his group is insightful. Ezra 8:16-17 describes Ezra's recruitment strategy: he sent for eleven men who would go to Casiphia, most likely a sanctuary or place of worship for the Jews around Babylon, to ask for Levites to accompany the journey (Breneman, 1993). Ezra's active role in this recruiting process is shown powerfully through his choice and preparation of the delegates. First, Ezra chose an impressive delegation to travel to Casiphia, calling nine leading men and two teachers. Kidner (1985) noted that it is no surprise to read of Ezra's careful choice of emissaries, "for he was looking for men who carried weight in the community and possessed the diplomatic skill to persuade and prepare the Levites who would make the trip" (p. 65). Allen (2003) detailed that Ezra needed Levites who were trained and prepared to lead worship as interpreters of the Torah, so his decision to send teachers, that is, experts in the Torah, to offer them a new job opportunity was essential to the delegation's success. Second, Ezra's task did not end with the selection of the delegation, but also with its preparation; Ezra 8:17 recorded that Ezra told his emissaries "what to say to Iddo and his brothers." In other words, Ezra briefed his team on who to look for and what to say; Fensham (1991) noted that the text literally reads that Ezra "placed in their mouths the words to say" (p.114). Thus, Ezra coached his team of delegates, a team specifically chosen because of their gifts and influence in the community, to go to Casiphia and recruit those who could serve Israel in leading the worship of God in the Temple.

The process worked remarkably for Ezra, as the recruiting team brought back thirty-eight Levites and 220 temple servants, including a "man of insight" and gifted leader, Sherebiah, leading Ezra to conclude that God's hand was upon the act (Ezra 8:18-20). Indeed, God's blessing can be seen in the addition of 220 temple servants, who were called the "given or dedicated ones". These servants, who traced their role back to the immigrants and prisoners of war procured through David's conquests in Israel, were foreigners that carried out the more menial tasks of temple worship (Kidner, 1985). Yamauchi (1988) commented on these temple servants: "Humanly speaking, the dedication of this group is remarkable. Socially they were a caste of mixed origins and were inferior to the Levites in status. But God's Spirit had motivated them to respond in larger number than the Levites" (p.659); Myers (1965) argued that it may have been their decision to join Ezra that persuaded the Levites to go as well.

For some, such a success in recruiting leaders would lead them to celebrate the accomplishments they had procured in their efforts, but not Ezra; sensing that God's hand had brought about the leaders he needed to continue, Ezra called the people to turn even more to God, proclaiming a fast in Ezra 8:21-23. The fast was carried out so that people might humble themselves before God to seek from Him a "safe journey for us, our little ones, and all our possessions." Ezra sought from God "a straight road" for the safety of his party, including "our little ones," which is normally taken to mean small children, but can be used in a wider sense to include the weaker returnees venturing on this journey, including women, children, and the aged (Fensham, 1991; Myers, 1965). As a pack made up of families with the treasures of the king and the people of Babylon, Ezra's band of returnees would have been very tempting bait for robbers, as grave dangers often faced those who traveled between Mesopotamia and Palestine (Yamauchi, 1988). While Ezra was aware of such danger, he was ashamed to ask for the king's assistance with a military escort, for in the course of securing the mission to restore worship at the temple, Ezra had told the king, "The hand of our God is favorably disposed to all those who seek Him, but His power and His anger are against all those who forsake Him" (Ezra 8:22). After making known that God was the protector of His people, Ezra was not willing to waver from this confession; instead, he led the people to fast and seek God concerning their safety. The incredible result was summarized in Ezra 8:31, when the people saw

God's hand deliver them from the hand of the enemy and ambushes along the way.

As we consider how Ezra recruited and trained leaders in this opening vignette, three leadership behaviors emerge from his example. First, Ezra's acknowledgement of a need for leaders came as the result of inspecting his people and knowing the task for which they were called. With a clear mission of calling the people of Israel back to the rightful worship of God in His temple, Ezra knew he would need Levites who could lead the people in that very task. His call for leaders was not a broad call for help, but rather, a very specific search for the people whom God had gifted to serve in God's design.

But it was not enough to acknowledge a need for leaders; Ezra proceeded to recruit those who could fill such need. Ezra's strategy in recruiting leaders is noteworthy, as he did not personally recruit the Levites he sought after; rather, he selected appropriate recruiters and trained them properly. As the leader of the traveling party consisting of hundreds of people, it would have been difficult for Ezra to personally recruit the leaders he would need, but in working with others who could serve as his delegates, Ezra was able to find the leaders needed to carry out God's work while remaining faithful to his leadership post. Further, Ezra's attention to detail in choosing the proper delegation and training them prepared the delegates to carry out the task they were commissioned for and return with the leaders needed for the journey. By making his expectations clear, the recruiters were able to enlist the candidates who best met the need of the congregation.

Finally, Ezra's consistency in trusting God to provide for the journey, both through the provision of leaders and the protection of the traveling party, drew the people closer to God as they sought Him in fasting and prayer. The Christian leader's activities are always carried out with an eye toward teaching God's people about the God they serve; in trusting God to protect those who seek Him, even in the face of imminent danger, Ezra demonstrated to the returning exiles the nature of their God and led them to praise the One who delivered them. Further, prayer is seen, not as a luxury, but as a necessity in the recruiting and preparation of leaders. Ezra found the workers who would serve God by bowing before God's throne.

In summary, a look at Ezra's leadership in Ezra 8 reveals these cardinal leadership behaviors:

- Ezra recruited for specific roles with clear expectation of duties.

- Ezra selected and trained a team of recruiters to help in the enlistment process.
- Ezra bathed the recruitment process in prayer.

How Pastors Can Lead in Recruiting and Training Leaders

Organizations rise and fall based on the leadership that they employ and Sunday school is no different in this regard. The leaders that you recruit and train will either become your greatest blessings or your worst nightmares. Taylor (2009) said it best: "The significance of proper enlistment of your leaders cannot be overemphasized. If you fail at this point, then the other points have no significance" (p.36). In general, recruiting and training are two sides of the same coin. Parr (2002) argued that most churches struggling to recruit leaders have a training problem, as current leaders are often not equipped to explain their roles or train others in how to carry out their work. Following the same line of thinking, Hunt (1997) noted that the best recruiting shows people how to do the task they are being recruited for, linking the two tasks together from the start. Pritchett (2013) argued that a well thought-out strategy to continuously recruit and train leadership must be in place to keep the Sunday school focused and vibrant, agreeing with Parr's (2010) finding that a regular training program was the most common factor among the fastest growing Sunday schools in

Georgia Baptist churches.

Yet, pastors are not left in the dark when it comes to leading recruitment and training practices in Sunday school. Ezra's model provides an excellent example for three categories of behaviors that pastors can use to lead their Sunday school to recruit well and train in a manner that develops leaders to grow as disciples of Christ and leaders of the flock.

Pray for Potential Leaders

The pastor should begin the recruitment and training of Sunday school leaders with prayer. Hemphill (1996) declared, "If your church has a leadership problem, it may actually be a prayer problem," calling pastors to make leadership recruitment a matter of churchwide prayer (p.143). Parr (2010), calling for leaders to pray fervently and regularly for God to raise up leaders, asks the probing question, "Are you praying for God to raise up and call out leaders within your class? Are you really?" (p.114). In discussing how to find kingdom leaders, Hemphill and Taylor (2001) similarly advise to begin with prayer, concluding that "God will guide you to the right people. After all, he has a vested interest in the success of your church" (p. 81-82).

While it is no surprise to see prayer listed as a first step, it is not done so just for the sake of sounding spiritual; it is a real battle in ministry to intentionally pray and seek the Lord in day to day decision making. How many times have we taken the Sunday school class lists and begin to pencil in the names of the best teachers or the most available workers without seeking the direction of the Lord or asking for His wisdom? Even now, my mind is brought back to two Sunday school recruiting attempts that went drastically different, due in large part to the difference in my willingness to pray. On one occasion, our church was blessed to have a teacher who was regularly a teacher of the year in our local school and was known to be an educational expert in the area. As happens from time to time, an opening came up in one of our Sunday school classes and, without even a bit of hesitation and nary a prayer, I asked the expert teacher to take the helm of the class, a position she was more than happy to take. While she was a wonderful teacher in terms of her techniques, it did not take long to realize that her view of Scripture was nowhere near that of our church and before long, I had to deal with a mutiny from this class. My rush to recruit without prayer led to many months of pain and conflict in our body.

But when we begin with prayer, we reorient ourselves to the will of God and we begin to consider who the Holy Spirit is preparing and calling to lead His people rather than who will simply meet the need of the moment. On another occasion, I was presented with an adult class whose teacher sadly passed away quickly. The class was left without a teacher, but rather than jump to fill the spot quickly, I decided that I would fill in and we would commit as a class to pray for God to raise up the teacher He was calling to lead them in their study of His Word. As we prayed weekly for this teacher, we began to have one of the students volunteer to share teaching duties with me for the class. This lady had not been a teacher before, but as she experienced teaching first hand and continued in prayer, she decided to follow the Lord's leading to teach the class. The result? Years later, she continues to faithfully teach God's Word and the class has continued to serve as a powerful witness for Christ, both within their church and in the community around them.

What are some practical ways that you can lead your Sunday school in prayer, though? One easy starting point is to simply ask your congregation to pray for leaders and lead them in such prayers in your worship services; this is a great way to publicly involve your church in seeking the Lord for Sunday school leaders. Asking classes to dedicate a week each month to praying for new leaders can be a helpful habit to form in classes as well; my classes would always dedicate a moment or two on the first Sunday of each month to prayer for their leaders and for God to call new leaders, making it a constant reminder to lift up their leaders before the Lord. Finally, praying for future Sunday school leaders can be a special task for you to take to your prayer warriors who may not be able to get involved in ministry as easily; one of my fondest memories as a pastor was visiting a dear shut-in who would weekly pray for God to raise leaders in her church and Sunday school! The key to leading your church to pray for new leaders is to model it yourself as a pastor; if you are not praying for Sunday school leaders, oftentimes those who follow you will not either.

Select and Train a Group of Recruiters

Many pastors' eyes will undoubtedly begin to roll as they consider experiences of working with nominating committees; Taylor's (2009) caution that a general churchwide nominating committee often does not have the ability to adequately staff all the positions of the church looms large, though many churches continue the practice. Yet, we saw in Ezra's example that enlisting a group of recruiters can be a powerful tool for the wise leader, as they are able to commission others to strategically seek prospective leaders while focusing on their leadership post. But perhaps the most important piece of this puzzle is found in the pastor's involvement in recruiting Sunday school leaders who are aware of the expectations and requirements of the task to serve as recruiters: "Sunday school leaders should enlist Sunday school teachers and workers because this will be the team with which he must work.... The principle is simple; if you have no input into your personnel, you are not the team leader" (Taylor, 2009, p.137). Indeed, in training your recruiters on the types of leaders they should seek, you are setting the tone for the expectations you have for leaders and making it clear which direction you would like to see your Sunday school moving towards.

This may sound overwhelming at first, but the practice is relatively simple for a pastor to get involved with. In working with your Sunday school leaders, you will find some who truly understand the vision and the aim of your program; it is these leaders who you will ask to help you, reminding them of your central values and asking them to look and pray for those who would be teachable and willing to continue working toward the goal of teaching the Bible, caring for one another, and taking the gospel out to the lost. Pray with these recruiters and guide them toward people you have noticed that may be able. As Ezra led his team to seek out Iddo and his men, you should also be on the lookout for people you can suggest for your team and take an active role in talking to these prospective leaders.

Recruit for Specific Roles with Clear Expectations

How many times have you sat in a church meeting where you heard someone beg for volunteers to "just come and help us out" with little direction and little definition? I still chuckle when I think of my son, Nate, leaning over and telling me, "those babies must be rough," after an exasperated nursery worker made a general call for someone to help! While it may seem that the easiest method of recruiting leaders is to make a mass call from the pulpit for Sunday school workers, Parr (2002) noted that it rarely works, as many assume that you are talking about someone else. Rather, as Ezra demonstrated, it is much more effective to recruit with a specific role in mind. Recruiting for a specific position or role allows the recruiter to approach the prospective worker with a clear picture of the task they are being asked to consider; "People are more likely to serve if they know that the church will provide them the resources and necessary training" (Hemphill, 1996, p.116).

Recruiting for specific roles, however, creates the need for clear expectations and standards of the role. Chapter six will cover how to develop standards for Sunday school leaders in more depth, but it is important at this point to note that clearly stated and defined expectations carry much power and influence in your enlistee, as

"Each leader needs to know exactly what is expected of him in order to properly go about performing the functions of his responsibilities" (Taylor, 2003, p.17). The key principle for pastors is to realize that we are not just asking for anyone; we are asking for specific leaders to carry out specific roles. Instead of asking, "Who wants to help?", we would be much better served to seek the Lord and ask specific people, "Will you join us in this role?"

As we prepare to move into Ezra 9 and 10 and see how the task of accountability often arises for the leader, it would be helpful to remember how recruiting leaders led Ezra to respond. Having seen the Lord work in leading Levites to his band of exiles, Ezra called on the people to humble themselves before the Lord and prepare for the journey ahead of them (Ezra 8:21). The recruitment process had not been a draining experience, nor one of dread, but rather, it became a worship experience, as Ezra and the people were able to see God's power and wisdom at work, guiding the hearts of the Levites and providing His people with the leaders necessary for them to restore worship in Jerusalem. In the same way, as we cover our recruiting in prayer, work with faithful leaders, and develop clear standards and roles, we must keep in mind that the Lord is working amongst us and positioning His people in the places that He has gifted them to serve for His glory. While the recruiting process can easily become a drudgery, it can also serve as a powerful tool to lead us and our churches to see God's might and to worship; the choice as to which it will be rests in your hands!

Questions for Discussion
1. What are some of the insights you gained from considering how Ezra recruited and trained leaders?
2. What are some ways that you can encourage your Sunday school to pray for leaders as a pastor?
3. What are some of the advantages of working with a group to recruit leaders? What are some of the disadvantages?
4. Why is it important to recruit with specific roles in mind?

A Chance for Deeper Thought

Recruiting leaders is not an easy task, even for the most experienced of leaders, but as Ezra demonstrated, a process bathed in prayer can turn the task into a worship experience. Leading a church to pray for Sunday school and its leaders is an essential part of this process for a pastor. Construct a 1-2 page prayer guide to help direct your church in how to pray for Sunday school and its leadership; include Bible verses and biblical examples of how they may pray.

4

DEALING WITH A MESS

Recruiting and training leaders can be exciting work! It is a great day when people respond and commit to becoming a Sunday school leader. Some of the greatest days in ministry come from seeing people you have recruited and trained flourish in the work of teaching God's Word, caring for God's people, and taking the gospel out into the world. Seeing the hard work of recruiting bear fruit is thrilling; seeing the effort you have put into training begin to put down roots in leaders' lives brings unbelievable joy and is a real encouragement to both the pastor and the church!

While it is important to recruit and train the leaders God is preparing around you, the next piece of Ezra's story reminds us that it is equally important to call those leaders to follow God's standards. Pastors must consistently call those who lead with them to represent God in their work and follow His ways. In other words, if the leaders are not committed to following God's commands, how can they lead others to do so? This question is especially important in a volunteer setting like Sunday school, where availability and a willingness to serve often carries greater weight than the spiritual integrity a leader demonstrates.

In this chapter, we enter the tough discussion on how to deal with messes as a pastor leading Sunday school. While Ezra 8 demonstrated the scribe's leadership in recruiting and training leaders, the vignette presented in Ezra 9 and 10 looks at how Ezra handled a situation where the leaders were openly guilty of disobeying God's Word. If God's people are to follow God's standards, then the leaders who guide them must follow them first. But what happens when they do not?

A Look at How Ezra Guided Leaders to Follow God's Standards

Ezra 9 picks up the narrative of Ezra's work four and a half months after his return to Jerusalem (Ezra 10:9), when Ezra had turned to instructing the people in the knowledge of the Law. Typical of Ezra's leadership style, the scribe had sought to teach the Scripture and work with leaders rather than lead the work of restoring proper worship in the temple alone. As he taught, he was approached by some of the princes of the Jews in Ezra 9:1, leaders who were a part of the people already in the land when Ezra arrived. They had come to confess that a great sin had arisen in their midst: the leaders were engaged in mixed marriages.

"The people of Israel and the priests and the Levites have not separated themselves from the people of the lands, according to their abominations," the officials confessed in Ezra 9:1. The people and their leaders had taken wives from the Canaanites, the Hittites, the Perizzites, the Jebusites, the Ammonites, the Moabites, the Egyptians, and the Amorites; in doing so, "the holy race has intermingled with the people of the lands," and rather than helping with the issue, "the hands of the princes and the rulers have been foremost in this unfaithfulness" (Ezra 9:2). The substance of the confession is that the members of the religious community had both married into and adopted some of the religious practices of the rest of the Palestinian population (Williamson, 1985). Kidner (1979) explained that Ezra's campaign to teach the Torah to the people had "thrown new light not only on a tolerated evil but on the high calling of this community as a *holy race*" (p.68, emphasis in the original).

This problem may seem odd in our contemporary setting and it would be easy to conclude that the problem of mixed marriages is a problem of racism on the part of the Jews, but Fensham (1991) noted that this was far from the truth, as the prohibition against marrying the people of the land came from a concern for the purity of the religion of the Lord; for instance, "the influence of a foreign mother, with her connection to another religion, on her children would ruin the pure religion of the Lord and would create a syncretistic religion running contrary to everything in the Jewish faith" (p.124). Thus, the true problem underlying such marriages was the question of religious identity, leading Fensham (1991) to conclude, "it was a question of the living relation between the Lord and his people, and not of who one's ancestors might be" (p.125).

An interesting insight into how Ezra's role as instructor of the Torah played a part in the leaders' confession can be seen in the leaders' understanding of their iniquity. While the claims of Ezra 9:1-2 seem direct in their allegation of wrongdoing, Williamson (1985) noted that a sophisticated exegetical approach to the Law underlies the claim, as this is not the direct quoting of a single command, but rather, an application drawn from several passages throughout the Law. Thus, laws prohibiting marriage with the indigenous population of Canaan (e.g. Exodus 34:11-16; Deuteronomy 7:1-4; 20:10-18) are now interpreted by reference to the contemporary "peoples of lands," not based on their ethnicity, but because of their abominations. Williamson (1985) concluded that the chiefs' confession "thus betrays an advanced level of exegetical reflection on several legal texts. This again may point to the nature of Ezra's teaching ministry during the preceding months" (p.131).

Ezra's Response to the Confession of the Leaders

While Ezra's teaching may have led the leaders to realize their failure to follow the Law, it was the leaders who brought the matter to the attention of their teacher; his response can be seen in Ezra 9:3-15. Upon hearing the news, Ezra tore his clothes, pulled hair from his head and his beard, and sat appalled, mourning the sin reported publicly before the people. The sins of the leaders had been brought into public knowledge and Ezra's chagrin was clearly reflected in his self-abasement before the temple, but this act was more than personal disappointment; "Ezra was, in a sense, an embodiment of the word of God to the people. Around him congregated a group of disloyal exiles whom he led into a service of confession at the time of the evening sacrifice" (Myers, 1965, p.78). Allen (2003) explained that "Ezra engaged in ritual mourning that reflected extreme crisis. In the context it was meant to indicate repentance.... He was acting on behalf of the community and implicitly urging them to follow His example" (p.74). Kidner (1979) concluded that "Ezra's reaction was typical of him. It was almost inaction, yet more potent than any flurry of activity, since it drew out of other people the initiatives that could best come from them" (p. 68).

Ezra's response was certainly not left unnoticed, as Ezra 9:4 indicates that "everyone who trembled at the words of the God of Israel on account of the unfaithfulness of the exiles gathered to me." The people, knowing the demands of the law of God, stood trembling with Ezra, mourning for several hours until the time for the evening sacrifice arrived, an appointed time for prayer and confession. Ezra arose in Ezra 9:5, fell on his knees, and spread out his hands to God, "to make confession of the heavy guilt of the congregation before God, and thus impressively to set their sins before all who heard his prayer" (Keil, 1996, p.74).

The ensuing prayer that Ezra offered in Ezra 9:6-15 stands as one of the great prayers of confession in the Scriptures. He began by identifying himself with those who committed the sin in Ezra 9:6-7, crying out that he was ashamed and embarrassed to lift his face before God, for "our iniquities have risen above our heads and our guilt has grown even to the heavens." He recalled the suffering that Israel's sins had brought upon herself in the past and how Israel had been handed over into captivity (Ezra 9:7), bondage (Ezra 9:8), and slavery (Ezra 9:9). In other words, "he had a high sense of the glory they had betrayed, and he could not be reconciled to what they had become" (Kidner, 1965, p.69).

Yet, God's grace was ever before Ezra's eyes, for despite her sin, God had allowed a remnant of Israel to remain (Ezra 9:8) and gave her less punishment than she deserved (Ezra 9:13). In His mercy, God had given the people a "peg in His holy place" (Ezra 9:8), a reminder that since "the nomad can pitch his tent only where he has the right to do so," God had given the people a place to call home (Fensham, 1991, p.129-130). But even in the midst of this grace, Ezra realized that these gifts were a mere shadow of the things which God could do and give, for God granted them "a little reviving in our bondage" and "some reviving to raise up the house of our God" (Ezra 9:8-9).

Such recognition of God's graciousness to a people largely undeserving led Ezra to consider the present sin at hand in Ezra 9:10-12. To make the point clear to those listening in to his prayer, Ezra quoted a number of Scriptures in Ezra 9:11-12; Williamson (1985) noted that a single passage is not prescribed, but rather, a mosaic of texts from Deuteronomy 7, 11, 23, 2 Kings 21, and Isaiah 1 are pieced together to show the unity of Scripture regarding the matter. This led Ezra to a clear recognition in Ezra 9:13-15 that the people deserved for God to turn away from them; they stood before a righteous God with nothing of value to present and God has every reason to wash His hands of the Jewish community. Kidner (1979) concluded well that, "Ezra had not even the heart to plead, as Moses had, that God's name would suffer in such a case. His prayer was naked confession, without excuses, without the pressure of so much as a request" (p.69).

The People's Reaction to Ezra's Leadership

Taking root in his sincere humility, Ezra's confession and self-abasement spread among the people; Ezra 10 recorded the people's response to Ezra's public act of repentance. "Ezra has pricked their conscience to the point at which they now urge him to act" (Kidner, 1979, p.69-70). While Ezra was praying and making confession before the house of God, Ezra 10:1 reveals that a very large assembly of men, women, and children gathered to him and wept bitterly. Surely the wails of the mourners, combined with the crowd gathered around Ezra in his prayer, led the people to understand something dramatic was on the horizon; Williamson (1985) adeptly concluded, the scene "introduces a note of tragic gravity as it reminds the reader of the possible social consequences of the proceedings about to be initiated," foreshadowing the extreme measures which lied ahead (p.149).

Amid this great confession, Shecaniah, a layman and the son of Jehiel, arose to address the crowd in Ezra 10:2-4. As a descendant of the first group of exiles in Ezra 2, Shecaniah was well qualified to serve as a spokesman for the indicted group of Jews engaged in mixed marriages. While Shecaniah was not numbered among the guilty parties in Ezra 10, his father, Jehiel, was listed in Ezra 10:26 as one who had taken foreign wives; in other words, this was a matter of great importance that would have an impact on Shecaniah, both in his spiritual and familial relations.

Whereas Ezra's grief led him to tears, Shecaniah sees in Ezra's prayer a glimmer of hope. In verse 2, Shecaniah admitted with Ezra that the people had been unfaithful to their God in marrying the people of the land, "yet now there is hope for Israel in spite of this." Fensham (1991) summarized Shecaniah's sentiment well: "The logical outcome from the prayer of Ezra is that if the iniquity is removed, there would be forgiveness for their sin. God is righteous; he is a God of grace. Thus, there must be hope" (p.134). The course of action was clear in Shecaniah's eyes; he called the people of Israel to make a covenant with God to put away all their foreign wives and children according to God's law. Looking to the spiritual leader who provoked this repentance through his teaching of God's law, Shecaniah ended his statement in Ezra 10:4 with a charge to Ezra to "Arise! For this matter is your responsibility, but we will be with you; be courageous and act." Ezra's time to lead had come, as "Shecaniah gave a clarion call to action. Weeping was not enough. Courageous and painful decisions had to be made. The people themselves had to respond" (Yamauchi, 1988, p.669).

Ezra's actions in Ezra 10:5-8 reveal both the decisive leadership and responsive spiritual life that had come to characterize his service as Israel's scribe. Immediately in verse 5, Ezra rose and placed the leading priests, Levites, and all of Israel under oath that they would carry out Shecaniah's proposal. "By making the people swear to follow the suggested course of action while feelings were still running high, Ezra ensured that there could be no turning back at a later stage" (Williamson, 1985, p.151). Having witnessed the leaders' commitment, Ezra withdrew from the crowd in verse 6 and retired to Jehohanan's chamber to fast and pray in mourning over the unfaithfulness of the people. In this, Ezra demonstrated that his earlier public mourning was not merely for show but was from a sincere and contrite heart; his prayers and actions were a part of His own walk with the Lord.

The result of Ezra's direction can be seen in verses 7 and 8, where the leaders issued a proclamation that all the exiles should assemble at Jerusalem within three days. This decree is interesting, as it does not come from Ezra himself, but rather, from the leaders and elders of the people. While Artaxerxes had granted Ezra the power to confiscate property, imprison the guilty, or even execute lawbreakers in Ezra 7:26, Ezra relied on the local leaders to enforce judgment rather than using the king's resources. Such a move showed the prowess of the scribe, as Kidner (1979) noted that the order (or counsel, as in verse 3) of the local leaders would carry more moral weight than mere imperial decrees. Further, if one should not attend, all his possessions would be forfeited and he would be excluded from the assembly of Israel; clearly, the gravity of the offense had not escaped the leaders, who acted with great haste to gather the people of Israel in Jerusalem.

The threat of these sanctions was apparently enough to win the people's full cooperation, as all the men assembled at Jerusalem within three days in Ezra 10:9-15. Allen (2003) captured the setting of the moment: "The weather could hardly have provided a more fitting background for the grim occasion. It was December, in the season of the early rains, and up in Jerusalem it was cold and miserable at the open-air meeting" (p.80). Verse 9 mentioned that the people stood before the house of God trembling, both because of the matter at hand and the heavy rains. Calling the people's attention once more to their sin in verse 10, Ezra gave the call to action in verse 11: "make confession to the Lord God of your fathers and do His will; and separate yourselves from the peoples of the land and from the foreign wives."

While the message had been heard, the execution would be difficult, leading to the people asking Ezra to set up a committee to investigate the matter to see who is guilty in Ezra 10:12. Their request was not an attempt to escape the application of the command, but rather, a reasonable entreaty considering the context; Fensham (1991) detailed that the large crowd, unfavorable weather conditions, and the sheer bulk of cases that needed to be decided would make the prospect of a one day judgment untenable, as a rush to draw hasty conclusions and to commit an injustice to people would also be unwise. The solution, then, was to appoint chiefs who would hear the cases of families at set times and determine if they are guilty of mixed marriage "until the fierce anger of our God on account of this matter is turned away from us" (Ezra 10:14). While some opposed this delay in Ezra 10:15, nonetheless, the plan moved forward and a committee made up of family heads set about to execute Ezra's command.

Concerning the legal proceedings in Ezra 10:16-17 and the subsequent report in verses 18-44, Kidner (1979) wrote, "The fact that the hearings took three months proved the wisdom of having second thoughts about settling everything in a day or two and in a crowd. But it also showed how far the trouble had spread" (p.71-72). The work was a serious venture concerning the makeup of whole families, so care was needed to judge accurately. Using the list of one hundred and ten guilty men in verses 18-44, Fensham (1991) noted that the committee spent seventy-five days completing their tasks, meaning they may have only investigated two cases a day. While it is possible that some of the investigations ended with the accused being found innocent, the pace nonetheless reflects the care with which this work was carried out.

In listing the report of those found guilty, Ezra 10:18-44 uses a top-down approach, beginning with the family of the high priest and descending to the priests, Levites, temple workers, and the people in general. While one might have expected the writer to gloss over the sins of the priests, this order highlights the fact that the leaders of the people in the worship of God are among the guilty (Kidner, 1979). Beginning with those among the high priest's family, Ezra 10:19 laid out the response of the guilty: they pledged to put their wives away and offered a ram as their guilt offering. Fensham (1991) expanded on the guilt offering made to expiate their sins, noting that the guilt offering described in Leviticus 5:14-26 referred to unintended transgression; if this was the case here, these marriages were regarded as unintentional acts. While this may be surprising among the priests, the apparent ignorance of sin regarding these marriages underscores the need for Ezra's instruction concerning the law, both for the leaders and the people. Verse 44 ended the listing of the convicted with the mention that all of these had married foreign wives, some of whom bore children, highlighting the tragic reality that sin had even torn apart families in Israel. Kidner's (1979) conclusion was a somber reminder, "On this painful note the story of Ezra's ministry breaks off. It is appropriate enough. His mission was to apply the law to his people (7:14), and the law brings the knowledge of sin" (p.72). In the end, Ezra's leadership in Ezra 9 and 10 reveals three more leadership behaviors for pastors as they lead Sunday school:

- Ezra taught God's standards for living to the leaders and the people.
- Ezra responded to the leaders' sin with a call for confession and repentance.
- Ezra worked with the leaders of the people to fairly adjudicate the cases of sin and broken standards.

How Pastors Can Call Leaders to Follow God's Standards

In any group of people, leaders are tasked with carrying out a number of roles. Often, they are masters of the group's culture, training followers in the ways to live and function in the group; other times, they are directors, guiding followers to the appropriate context to apply their skills and talents and ensuring that all tasks are being completed. But leaders are always role models; the leader's example and behavior sets the tone for how the followers perceive the group and how they understand the values of the group. This was certainly the case with Ezra as he handled a very messy situation in the lives of the returning exiles.

But what can pastors learn from Ezra's leadership to help them lead Sunday school? Of all the leadership behaviors we can observe in Ezra's life, these are the thorniest parts of the pastor's journey. If your experience in ministry is like mine, merely thinking about the need to hold leaders accountable to God's standards brings back painful memories of moral and spiritual failings that disqualified coworkers and friends in ministry, not to mention the subsequent fallout that their churches experienced in the aftermath. While this helps us to see the seriousness of the matter, it does not make the task any easier for pastors, as Taylor (2009) described the Sunday school leader's tightrope walk when it comes to expectations: "If the leader has no expectations, then he falls off one side of the tightrope. If his expectations are too unrealistic, then he falls off the other side of the tightrope! Welcome to the world of Sunday school leadership!" (p.93)

Ezra is the exemplar model of the faithful Bible teacher, as his actions were in line with his scholarship, a truth that pastors should lead Sunday school leaders to understand. Sunday school leaders will not know how to live by God's standards unless they know what God's standards are, meaning that accountability can only go as far as the faithful teaching of the Word. Consider the example of Ezra in this chapter: the recognition of sin and calls for repentance only came after several months of daily Bible teaching. A commitment to faithful teaching and preaching of Scripture sets within the culture of a church the expectation that believers will know and follow God's standard of living. We will look later in the book at the concept of leadership covenants and reasonable expectations to place on Sunday school leaders, but as a pastor, the greatest ways to help your Sunday school leaders know how Christ's disciples should live and lead is to teach them the Scriptures and live them out for yourself. More is often caught than taught, but the wise pastor will work to make sure that his words and his actions speak the same language and teach the same lesson.

Yet, even when we consistently teach and live the Scriptures, we cannot force someone to turn away from sin; it is inevitable that you will deal with a leader who has chosen to act against God's standards. Do not be surprised, pastor, when you face a Sunday school teacher who has chosen to engage in an extramarital affair, a care group leader who is arrested for driving under the influence, or an outreach leader that curses out a church member in the parking lot; as much as we wish it would not be the case, we still have to wrestle with sin and the flesh. But as we saw above with

Ezra, there is a proper response for pastors as they shepherd their Sunday school teachers. At the discovery of the public sin in Ezra 9 and 10, the scribe mourned before the Lord and led the people to confess their sin and repent, coming down to their level and identifying with them as a fellow sinner rather than as their judge. The goal of holding Sunday school leaders to God's standards is not to create a legalistic environment, but rather, to create a place where God is represented accurately. As such, all acts of accountability should be viewed with an eye toward reconciliation and repentance. As much as possible, pastors should use discipline to restore a fallen leader to favor with God with an eye toward God's grace; though he may be disqualified from leadership positions for a time, such encouragement may help the leader avoid being hardened by the deceitfulness of sin (Hebrews 3:13) and allow for reconciliation with God.

Serving as a Sunday school leader is a commitment to leading and shepherding God's people, a task that should be taken seriously; "Leaders must shoulder the functions of their positions. If a teacher does not carry the responsibilities of his position, then he has forfeited his right to occupy the position" (Taylor, 2003, p.73). Removing a Sunday school leader from his post, though, is not a popular action and should be handled with grace and forethought, as many pastors have been dismissed from their churches on account of disciplinary actions handled poorly. In this regard, pastors are wise to follow the advice of Hemphill and Taylor (2001) to form and work with a team of Sunday school leaders to develop clear expectations of leaders and spell out plainly any disciplinary actions that may be taken and who will judge whether an offense has taken place. Much as Ezra enlisted family chiefs to lead in the investigation of the marriages in Ezra 10, so should pastors look to mature leaders who can act with discretion and discernment to serve as an advisory panel that ensures that discipline is not arbitrary and that such actions are in line with Scripture. The wise pastor will make sure that principal church leaders are aware of both the expectations and the disciplinary measures.

Though he was considering the work of Sunday school in general, Taylor's (2009) reminder serves pastors well in this regard:

> People bring messes as they have problems, issues, and sin. Sometimes it can get real ugly, but this is the work God has called us to. It is dirty work…. Livestock brings value to the farmer but also drops plops all around the barn. Clean barns require the elimination of livestock that bring profit. So it is with people; they bring both value and messes to church. Somebody has got to help them through their messes. (p.31-32)

As a pastor, you will often be forced to deal with messes: with leaders, with church members, even within yourselves. We live in a fallen and broken world where we are subjected to the consequences of both our sin and others' sins regularly. But the Lord offers His grace to us, even in our failings; 1 John 1:8-9 says, "If we say that we have no sin, we are deceiving ourselves and the truth is not in us. If we confess our sins, He is faithful and righteous to forgive us our sins and to cleanse us from all unrighteousness." Faithfully teaching God's Word and making clear the standards of a holy life to leaders will help to keep leaders away from sin, while working with mature leaders to call fallen leaders to confession and repentance will bring restoration and encourage the believers that God is faithful. But in the end, the greatest thing that a pastor can do in calling leaders to follow God's standards is to follow them himself. Just as Ezra began by studying the Word, doing it, and teaching it, so we as pastors must be faithful to study the Word and apply it, letting God shape our lives and our teaching as we walk with Him.

While the first two vignettes of Ezra's leadership were primarily concerned with his guidance of leaders, both in recruiting leaders and calling leaders to follow God's standards, the next vignette demonstrates how Ezra taught the people the Word of God personally. Though the book of Ezra seemingly faded into the pain of dissolving marriages and families, some thirteen years later, Ezra would emerge again from the background in Nehemiah 8 to lead the people in the reading of the Law; as Kidner (1979) remarked, "a postscript will follow, when Ezra will present the positive and festive aspects of the law: its gift of light to the mind, and its witness to God as liberator and provider" (p.72). While removing the cancer of sin is often painful, the fruit of its removal is a healthy body that can enjoy the goodness that God provides. If you are willing to put in the tough work of calling Sunday school leaders to follow God's standards and holding them accountable to clear out the impurity of sin, the fruit of a pure body focused on Christ will bring joy indeed!

Questions for Discussion

1. What did you learn about Ezra's view of sin in light of his response in Ezra 9?
2. What difficulties do you see in calling leaders to follow God's standards for living?
3. What are some ways that pastors can teach God's standards for living to their leaders?
4. Is it ever appropriate to ask someone to step down as a Sunday school leader? Why or why not?

A Chance for Deeper Thought

Holding Sunday school leaders accountable to live by God's standards is not popular in today's churches. In my study of Georgia Baptist Church senior pastors (Smith, 2014), most pastors (69%) strongly agreed that it is important for pastors to discipline Sunday school leaders who violate God's standards and nearly all pastors (96%) considered themselves as responsible for holding Sunday school leaders accountable. Yet, only 36% of all churches in that study had a written set of standards that defined the standards and expectations of Sunday school leaders. In a 2-3 page essay, make a list of what you believe should be basic expectations of a Sunday school leader's Christian walk and lifestyle based on Scripture and reflect on what that list teaches you about your own walk with Christ.

5

BRING OUT THE BOOK

Sometimes, you just do not get to do what you planned on doing. It is an all too common occurrence for a pastor's schedule to be delayed by a church member's surgery, an urgent counseling need, or even just a surprise water leak in the church office! There are any number of things that take a pastor away from the work of teaching and preaching God's Word and that is alright; after all, we have committed to care for and shepherd God's flock. However, it is also daunting for many who entered the pastorate with the dream of preaching and teaching all the time, only to find that they often must sneak in time to be able to study and prepare for the task.

This is not a new phenomenon, though, for we can see in our walk through the scenes of Ezra's ministry that the scribe often experienced the same amendments to his schedule. The man who set his heart to study God's Word, do it, and teach it to those in Israel was called upon to lead a group of exiles from Babylon to Jerusalem, requiring him to recruit and train his own leaders. Even more, after Ezra had settled and begun to teach the Word, he was presented with a nationwide sin that needed to be addressed. While his calendar surely did not include a 75-day investigation of the marriages of Israel's tribal leaders, Ezra followed the leading of the Lord in all these cases as he walked with Him, just as pastors must in our day.

But as we follow Ezra's story into the book of Nehemiah, we finally see the scribe doing the work of teaching God's Word as we come upon a much improved and nearly rebuilt Jerusalem. The Lord had sent the charismatic Nehemiah, to lead the people to rebuild and repopulate the city, a task they carried out in breathtaking speed. As the doors to the city gates were hung in Nehemiah 7, the people of Israel gathered outside of Jerusalem, for it was the important seventh month of the Jewish calendar. Falling around the end of September through the beginning of October, this was a time of feasts and solemn assemblies, with regulations laid out for the people in Leviticus 23. The first day of the seventh month began the New Year for the Jews with the Feast of Trumpets, a time for the people to rest from their labor and present an offering unto the Lord. This was followed by the Day of Atonement on the tenth day, and the month ended with the Feast of Booths, which began on the fifteenth of the month and lasted seven days before it was completed on the eighth day with a holy convocation before the Lord.

So, Nehemiah 8 opens with the people gathered together at the square, asking Ezra to "bring the book of the Law of Moses which the Lord had given to Israel" (Nehemiah 8:1). "Ezra now emerges from obscurity, and it is typical of him that he has quietly waited to be asked for" (Kidner, 1979, p.104); the time has now come for Ezra to take the stage once again, this time for the purpose of teaching the people God's Word. As we look into Nehemiah 8, we will be able to consider how Ezra taught the people God's Word, leading them to a renewed fellowship with God and the knowledge of how He is to be worshipped.

How Ezra's Teaching of God's Word Led to a Renewed Fellowship with God

In Nehemiah 8:1-12, we see the people gathered together on the first day of the seventh month in what Kidner (1979) termed as a "mood of rare responsiveness," as they gathered in unity (literally "as one man") in front of the Water Gate to hear Ezra read and teach the Law of Moses. The choice of venue is a revealing detail, as the Water Gate was found in the eastern wall of the city near to the Gihon Spring (Myers, 1965; Williamson, 1985) and not in the temple courts, where only men could enter; this was meant to be an assembly for everyone. Kidner (1979) explained that this assembly was not held around the altar, but rather, in the center of city life, "the kind of place where God's wisdom pleads most urgently to be heard... The law itself insisted that its voice must not be confined to the sanctuary but heard in the house and in the street" (p. 105).

Though he had been called upon by the people to bring out the book of the Law, this was not a spontaneous gathering as Nehemiah 8:4 describes that Ezra emerged with 13 other men onto a wooden podium that had been built just for the occasion. The only detail given about the thirteen men standing with Ezra is their names, leading many commentators to believe they must have been influential lay leaders or elders of the people, as no title (such as Levite or priest) is attached to their name (Breneman, 1993; Myers, 1965). Williamson (1985), supporting the idea that these men were laymen tasked with assisting Ezra with the reading of the Law, argued that, "Coupled with the choice of location, Ezra was boldly proclaiming that the Torah was for all people, not just for a few privileged by either birth or particular ability" (p. 289). In short, the scene was set for a presentation of God's Word to all of God's people.

Ezra read from the book of the Law from early morning to midday, a span of over five hours, with Nehemiah 8:3 detailing that "all of the people were attentive to the book of the law." At the reading of the Word, the people rose and stood listening; Kidner (1979) detailed: "What is strikingly apparent is the royal reception given to the Word of God. This day was to prove a turning-point. From now on, the Jews would be known predominantly [as] 'the people of the book'" (p.106).

Brought to their feet in respect for the Word and to the ground in worship, the people received both the proclamation and explanation of the Scriptures. As Ezra read from the Law, thirteen Levites, listed in Nehemiah 8:7, began to circulate among the people, moving from group to group among the people to make sure they had understood what they had heard. They were translating the Hebrew language of the Law into the Aramaic tongue of the people and were literally "breaking up" the text and translating it for the purpose of understanding and interpreting it (Fensham, 1991). Myers (1965) noted that Ezra did not read the whole corpus of the Law, as he only read through the morning; instead, he read from the Law with the intent of helping the people to understand it. Thus, the text was broken down into sensible units, giving the opportunity for others to share the work of reading with Ezra and allowing Ezra to select the portions he deemed most appropriate; "Coupled with the ministry of the Levites, this all leads to the climax of this portion of the chapter, that the people 'understood the reading'" (Williamson, 1985, p.291).

Upon hearing the Law proclaimed and understanding its message, Nehemiah 8:9 recorded that the Jews began to weep and mourn. "The reading and interpretation of the law struck a responsive chord in the hearts of the people. They had either never heard it expounded so forcefully or had forgotten its demands," Myers (1965) explained, "In any case, the people were made aware of their failure to keep the law; and the threats contained therein indicated their jeopardy... Hence their reaction was a sign of sorrow and repentance" (p.154).

While this reaction is understandable, this was not the day to weep and mourn, for the Feast of Trumpets was to be a time of joy and celebration for the things the Lord had done for His people; it was a time of soothing aromas, not of bitter tears. Accordingly, the leaders declared to the people in Nehemiah 8:9-10, "This day is holy to the Lord your God; do not mourn or weep;" instead, they called the people to celebrate God's goodness and enjoy the finest fare that the Lord had provided them, sharing it with those who had no meal prepared as a sign of generosity and thankfulness. But this was not merely a time to throw a party, for the heart of this command was found in the reminder that the "joy of the Lord is your strength." Having seen their guilt and the punishment they deserved in the Law, the Israelites were to celebrate their identity as the people of God, for it was through this identification that they may receive the salvation promised in the Law; thus, the people were to celebrate in joy, for instead of receiving the judgment they deserved, the Lord would be their strength and their protection from destruction (Williamson, 1985).

With the calming help of the Levites, the message to celebrate in joy rather than mourn in sorrow was received and heeded and Nehemiah 8:12 records that all the people went away to carry out what the leaders had commanded. Perhaps the most important conclusion is found at the end of Nehemiah 8:12, where the people went to celebrate "because they understood the words which had been made known to them." Kidner's (1979) conclusion pointed to the significance of this moment: "To have *understood* what God was saying was what made the occasion. It was a step from blind righteousness towards some degree of divine-human fellowship" (p.107-108, emphasis in the original). Thus, in reading the Law to the people and guiding them to understand what God had said, Ezra and the leaders had brought the people closer to God and prepared their hearts to worship Him in the ways that He had commanded.

Ezra's public teaching in Nehemiah 8:1-12 offers many helpful guiding lights to a pastor's ministry today. We must not overlook Ezra's readiness for this moment, as Williamson (1985) described the scene of Nehemiah 8 as a "happy confluence of a congregation anxious to hear the Law of God read to them and a teacher willing to match their demands" (p.297). You will not always be blessed with a congregation that calls for the Word to be taught, much less one which stands in respect and falls in worship at its reading, but you can control your own effort. Your willingness to put in the work to study the Scriptures and to sharpen your own communication skills will help you clearly lay out God's Word for those who are ready and willing to listen.

While the response of the people is remarkable, Nehemiah 8:1-12 is a testament to a leader who was willing to take the task of training leaders seriously. The very Levites that Ezra recruited earlier were the ones at work explaining the Law among the people; in the same way, a pastor's proclamation of God's Word will often be filtered and explained through the work of Sunday school leaders. People will normally seek clarity from the ones they know and trust and often their most trusted biblical authorities are their Sunday school teachers; over the years, I have fielded scores of questions on previous sermons as a Sunday school teacher because my students trusted me. It is essential, then, that pastors prepare their Sunday school leaders to understand the Word and to teach it clearly, both in their modeling of how to study and teach the Word and in their training times. Taylor (2009) argued that "The standard for the Word of God is set in our churches first by the pastor and then by the teaching ministry of the church, which is the Sunday school" (p.76); as a pastor, you must understand that Sunday school leaders are extensions of your teaching ministry and invest in them properly.

Finally, the pastor would be wise to consider the power of the pulpit to serve as a platform. While he did expressly mention this, Ezra presented a clear message to the people that God's Word was applicable to all people and should be handled by all in his choice of venue and coworkers. In the same way, pastors often communicate more than their sermons contain in the way that they handle their platform. By the announcements he makes and the examples he uses, the pastor demonstrates what he values and what is important to the congregation. Just as Ezra involved laymen in the reading of the Word, so pastors can show their trust in their Sunday school leaders by recognizing them from the pulpit, referencing passages used in Sunday school, and serving as the chief encourager and champion for Sunday school.

How Ezra's Teaching of God's Word Led to a True Worship of God

Oftentimes, people do not realize how dehydrated they are until they taste the first drop of water; in the same manner, Ezra's teaching of God's word in Nehemiah 8:1-12 had not quenched the people's desire for a knowledge of God, but instead, served to whet their palates, leading to thirst for more of the Scriptures. The seventh month was an extremely busy time, as the religious feasts and assemblies took place in the prime days of the harvest, making time a precious commodity. Yet, the heads of the fathers of the people, along with the Levites and priests, on the heels of the public reading of the Law, recognized Ezra's skillful teaching and gathered around him the next day for a more intense study. They had gathered in Nehemiah 8:13 that "they might gain insight into the words of the Law," an expression that Kidner (1979) suggested meant more than a passive listening; they were seeking to follow God and lead their children to do the same, a task that required that they knew God's words and commandments.

As the leaders studied God's Word with Ezra, they found that they had not followed the Law concerning the celebration of the Feast of Booths. They had not neglected the Feast itself, as they had celebrated it in Ezra 3:4-6; rather, it was the method of celebration they had missed, as the people were called to live in booths during the seven days of the Feast. The feast was a celebration, not only of the harvest God provided, but of the God who had provided for His people, even during their wilderness trek. Living in booths was to be a reminder to the people of the history of God's people and a clear call to follow the Lord and not turn away.

The leaders' response in Nehemiah 8:15 points again to an advanced understanding and application of the Law, highlighting the effect of Ezra's teaching. The leaders issued a proclamation to all cities calling the people to go into the hills and bring various branches with them to Jerusalem, which they would use to build booths to live in throughout the celebration of the Feast of Booths. In Leviticus 23:42, there was no command as to how the booths were to be constructed, but in Nehemiah 8:15, Ezra and the leaders have determined that the building materials were to be made up of the branches of the various trees that the people were to bring (Lev. 23:40); Allen (2003) noted that this application shows the mark of interpretation, as the people were trying to understand and apply God's Law. Further, Williamson (1985) argued that the very act of circulating a proclamation reflects the peoples' understanding of Leviticus 23:2 and 4, where the people were called to proclaim the festivals at appointed times. Even more, the call to gather to Jerusalem seems to be influenced by the recapitulation of the commands concerning the Feast of Booth found in Deuteronomy 16:13-15, where the people are told to celebrate "in the place the Lord chooses." Noting that the influence of one passage on another ("Scripture interpreting Scripture") is a further characteristic of Ezra's exegesis, Williamson (1985) concluded that Nehemiah 8:15-18 demonstrates a further example of Ezra "making ancient Scripture practical and relevant for his own day" (p.295).

The people's response in Nehemiah 8:16-18 reveals that they carried out the commands of their leaders, making booths and gathering in the courts and squares of Jerusalem. There was great rejoicing throughout the whole assembly, as the people were worshipping in a way they had not since the days of Joshua by living in their booths (Neh. 8:17). Naturally, this led to the reading of God's law and the resulting solemn assembly in Nehemiah 8:18.

Thus, Nehemiah 8 ends in the way it began, with Ezra reading from the book of the Law to the assembly of Israel. Whereas the initial reading resulted in a renewed fellowship with God, the latter reading led the people to worship God in truth as He had commanded. Kidner (1979) remarked that the move to make Scripture the guiding principle of Jewish life had been powerfully initiated, for the public teaching of the word, the leaders' Bible study, and the reading of the Word throughout the festival "had exposed the people to the fundamentals of their faith with considerable thoroughness" (p.109). The people responded to the presentation of the Law in Nehemiah 8 with a great prayer of repentance in Nehemiah 9 and a new covenant to follow the ways of God in Nehemiah 10. Indeed, Ezra's commitment to read and teach the Law to the people had sparked a revival that led a band of exiles to return to their Lord and truly worship again as the people of God.

Just as Ezra's public teaching of the Word in Nehemiah 8:1-12 showed the value of Ezra's earlier work in recruiting and training Levites, the value of calling the leaders to follow the standards of God bore fruit in Nehemiah 8:13, as the same leaders who endured the drama of Ezra 9-10 were those who gathered around Ezra to gain insight into the words of the Law. By calling the leaders to take God's commands seriously, Ezra was able to teach the leaders and witness a great revival among the nation, as the people worshipped as they had not for centuries under their leaders' direction. While dealing with messes among Sunday school leaders is neither fun nor easy, it is often in these times of crises that pastors gain the authority and the trust from Sunday school leaders to serve as a credible teacher of God's Word. By responding to the crisis instead of avoiding it, you could be sowing the seeds of revival just as Ezra.

Finally, Ezra's willingness to teach his leaders personally in a small group setting cannot be understated. It is in a small group setting that people can ask questions and gain clarity over matters of Scriptures that they may not understand. While a pastor's willingness to support Sunday school publicly is important, there is no substitute for being involved personally, as Taylor (2009) noted that a pastor's willingness to join and attend a class "will send an unequivocal message to the entire congregation that Sunday school is important around here!" (p.134) The leaders gathered to Ezra to inquire of the Word, but Ezra was also ready and willing to teach the small group, a great example for pastors today.

Ezra's story ends on a triumphant note of sorts, as the scribe carried out the task he had set out for: to teach God's law and lead God's people to apply it to their lives. As we consider how Ezra led in Nehemiah 8, both in teaching the Word on a large, public scale, as well as teaching the Word in a smaller group setting, we see how the teaching of God's Word brought the people into a renewed fellowship with God and led them to worship anew. As such, Ezra demonstrated three more leadership behaviors that model how a pastor may lead Sunday school:

- Ezra personally proclaimed and taught God's word publicly to all people.
- Ezra trained and prepared leaders to help explain and apply God's word to the people.
- Ezra personally taught the Scriptures in small groups.

How Pastors Can Lead Sunday School By Teaching God's Word Personally

At first glance, it may seem that leading Sunday school by teaching God's Word would be the easiest of the leadership behaviors for pastors to use in their ministry. After all, many define the teaching of God's Word as a central task of a pastor. Yet in truth, despite first appearances, this may be the hardest part of leading Sunday school for most pastors.

It is true that recruiting leaders sometimes feels like a necessary evil and holding leaders accountable is always a drudgery, but these are tasks that go in cycles and spurts; they do not require week-to-week attention. Teaching God's Word personally, though, is a task that requires constant commitment and ongoing work. Whereas a leadership post can be filled or a fallen leader can be restored, the work of the Bible teacher is never finished, as we can always learn more about the Lord and learn to apply His Word more fully in our lives.

Leading from the Pulpit

Pastors do, however, have a good starting point available to lead Sunday school in teaching God's Word: their weekly preaching. It should come as no surprise that the people of Israel gained a renewed fellowship with God as they sat under Ezra's public proclamation of the Word, as the Lord Himself has declared that His Word will accomplish its purpose and will have success (Isaiah 55:11). Rainer (1999) noted that the teaching of God's Word through contextual preaching is one of the most powerful types of equipping approaches for churches: "As the Bible is taught in its context week after week through expository preaching, the Holy Spirit teaches the people and convicts them about their service and places of ministry" (p.17). While pastors may choose to deliver topical or thematic sermons from time to time in their ministry, the benefits of a regular expository preaching program can greatly aid the pastor in his goal of teaching God's word personally. Faithfully preaching the text of Scripture models the appropriate use and application of the Bible for Sunday school leaders and members and leads the congregation to follow God's ways in their lives. Parr (2013) concludes well: "God's word is the anchor of a healthy Sunday School. It is not enough to come together, but the body must be connected through the study of God's word as well as fellowship" (p.33).

But the pulpit also presents pastors with another opportunity to lead Sunday school, as it can serve as a platform for the pastor to speak as a leader. When I was a teenager, our pastor would often say, "God is good," and the church would respond, "All the time," followed by "All the time," "God is good." This might sound like a trivial chant, but it was a great example of the power of the pulpit as a platform, because the whole church was involved as a result of hearing the pastor saying this phrase over and over again. As one who proclaims God's Word, the pastor has been given authority in the church and is often looked to for direction and to understand the values of the church. While some pastors feel uncomfortable with this burden, the wise pastor will leverage this authority to encourage his church to seek the Lord and follow His ways.

As a leader of Sunday school, pastors can use the platform of the pulpit in powerful ways to encourage and strengthen his leaders. The mere mention of Sunday school leaders in introductions or sermon illustrations can encourage the leaders and show that the pastor supports them, an endorsement that often represents the whole church. Making note of Sunday school events or promotions from the pulpit shows leaders that the pastor is aware and involved in the program and that the events are worth mentioning. Simply announcing class times and locations or recognizing leaders and groups for achievements and victories communicates that the pastor values the work of Sunday school and is willing to trust others to lead. One of the fondest memories I have in ministry was a time when a dear lady came to me in tears, thanking me for supporting her and encouraging her as she led the care ministry in her Sunday school class. What had I done? I had only mentioned in our pastoral prayer time that she had visited one of our shut-in members after their surgery! Something as small as a mere mention may be the encouragement that God was seeking to give the leaders in your Sunday school.

Leading in Training

During one of my stops in ministry, I had the privilege of working with a retired NFL player on a weekly basis. Another NFL retiree had been recently fired as the coach of a small college team in our area and I asked my friend why the former player, who had been great as a professional, had not lasted long as a coach. His answer was simple: he had never learned how to coach what came naturally to him. Many pastors enter the ministry with a gifting in the area of Bible study or communicating biblical truths and seminary and Bible college training often further supplement these gifts. But teaching the Bible is quite different from teaching people how to teach the Bible, as there is a difference in teaching content as opposed to teaching a methodology or a skill. However, as we saw above with Ezra, it was by training others to teach the Word that all the people were able to understand it; a pastor must delegate, so training becomes a necessity.

The solution for this difficulty in training Sunday school leaders can be found in two major steps: organize and reach out. A consistent complaint among pastors and church leaders is a lack of attendance in training meetings, but often this is a result of a lack of organization and planning on the part of the trainers. Time is valuable and those who serve as Sunday school leaders in our churches also have responsibilities elsewhere, so one of the best ways to encourage attendance in training sessions is to schedule regular, ongoing meetings with clearly defined goals. When I served as an Education Pastor, we had our Second Sunday Night Sunday School Teacher meeting as a fixture on the church calendar; while I did not do a great job of coming up with a catchy title, it was memorable, and our teachers were able to build a routine to show up every Second Sunday Night of the month. You may have to start slower, using quarterly meetings rather than monthly, but having a simple plan and schedule will communicate the importance of the training to your leaders.

Above all, the greatest commitment a pastor can make to a regular training program is his own commitment to attend and take part in training sessions. The goal of a regular training program is to clarify the values of Sunday school and equip leaders with the skills and tools they need to carry those out. If, however, the Sunday school leaders see that the meeting is not valuable enough for the pastor to attend, they will not see Sunday school as a vital part of the church's ministry, but rather, as a program that the leaders of the church are not concerned with. This may sound harsh, but it is a reminder of the responsibility that a pastor holds as a leader of the church; if Sunday school training is important to a pastor, he needs to at least show up.

The second solution to helping a pastor deal with the difficulty of training Sunday school leaders is to reach out to those who can help with the training. Often, there are those in your church who have experience in lesson planning, organizing care groups, leading mission teams, or other skills you are seeking to train leaders in who would be able and willing to help you train or to even lead the training themselves. One of the most enjoyable times I had in Sunday school training came in a phenomenal lesson planning session that was led by a Teacher of the Year in our county who attended our church! Not only can you reach out within your church, but you can also reach out to sister churches around you or denominational agencies in your area. At another church I served in, a visionary youth pastor had noticed that many of the churches surrounding his did not have the funds to hire a youth minister, so he offered the youth workers of those churches to join him for training; because the churches were willing to reach out and accept help in training, the whole region grew in teaching God's Word, caring for His people, and sharing the gospel with the lost. If you still are struggling to find content for training, Parr (2010) suggested that a pastor could offer his leaders several resources to help in training, including: books, observing other teachers, attending seminars and conferences, and utilizing audio and video materials on teaching. No matter whether it is from people in your church, people around your church, or even published works, the willingness to reach out for help in training Sunday school leaders will demonstrate your commitment to your leaders and provide them with quality experiences to grow in their work for the

Kingdom.

While much more can (and has) been written about Sunday school training, I would like to offer one bit of advice for pastors who are just beginning to be involved in Sunday school training at your church. Organizing and reaching out for help in training are important factors to encourage Sunday school leaders to attend training and to understand that it is valuable, but an essential step for you as a pastor is to determine what your goal is in training. Thinking with the end in mind, your training sessions should help your leaders develop in their walk with Christ and equip them to lead in your Sunday school. The subject of your training sessions, then, should be related to the goals of your Sunday school. In chapter 2, we discussed the Four Stages of Group Development, which I use when I explain the goals and the values of Sunday school; as such, when I plan training sessions, each session relates to one of those stages. For instance, my first training session every year was on how to study the Bible to make a basic teaching plan, lining up with the Teach stage. Next, my second session covered how to hold class socials to get to know one another as part of the Care stage. The third session, in line with the Go stage, covered how to train your class to present their testimony of believing in Christ as a witnessing tool. Completing the circle, my fourth training session would cover how to identify and invest in apprentice teachers to prepare your group to reproduce. From there, I would continue to rotate around the circle, reinforcing those core values of Sunday school in the very training that equips it. You will not be able to fully train anyone in one session; after all, even Jesus spent several years with His disciples before He sent them out as leaders of the church. So, keep your expectations in check and set reasonable goals for your training sessions, teaching little bits at a time that line up with the goals of your Sunday school program and help your workers to grow in Christ.

Leading in Groups

As a part of my dissertation, I was given the opportunity to survey senior pastors in the Georgia Baptist Convention concerning their involvement in Sunday school leadership behaviors. While I was able to gain several insights through the study, one of the most surprising findings to me was that 40% of pastors admitted to not being involved in a Sunday school class at all (Smith, 2014, p.161). After leading many Sunday school training sessions for pastors over the years, I believe that, in truth, the percentage is much higher.

There are many reasons why pastors are not involved in Sunday school groups themselves. For some, their church's schedule makes it difficult, as multiple service times often means that Sunday school is taking place during a worship service, prohibiting a pastor from attending. For others, their workflow schedule interferes, as last-minute sermon preparations occur before their worship service, which is the time many Sunday schools take place. A surprising number of pastors have mentioned how their role as the pastor makes it hard for them to get involved in a group, as they are treated as the Bible answer man rather than a student or leader. Whatever the reason may be, many pastors have minimal to no involvement in Sunday school groups themselves.

But in so doing, they are missing an incredible opportunity to both lead Sunday school and to grow themselves. In calling pastors to join and attend a class, Taylor (2009) noted "His example will send an unequivocal message to the entire congregation that Sunday school is important around here!" (p.134). Further, Hunt (1997) reminded pastors that personally teaching small groups and Sunday school classes aids in the training process, as church members can watch them teach, work together in teaching, and eventually take on teaching themselves. Taking part in a Sunday school class, whether as a teacher or member, helps others to see that Sunday school is a value of the pastor and gives the pastor a group to support him and hold him accountable (Blanchard & Hodges,

2005). By participating in Sunday school, pastors are given another opportunity to emphasize that life change takes place through God applying His word to His people.

For those who are not involved in a group, I would like to suggest a three-step plan to begin leading. First, start in the hallways and show your presence to those coming to Sunday school. Being a greeter for those coming into Sunday school classrooms helps show that Sunday school is important to you and also gives you another chance to connect with your church members. Develop of a habit of dropping into a class each week and greeting the Sunday school leaders, telling them how you appreciate their work and encouraging them and their class. Even if your church schedule prohibits you from being in a group for a whole class, this ten-minute routine just before Sunday school will do wonders for the morale of your leaders.

Second, find a way to get involved in a Sunday school group! Not only will this help to demonstrate your commitment as a leader, but even more so, it will help you grow in your walk with the Lord as you study God's Word, care for His people, and share the gospel with others. Pastors are so often looked to as the dispenser of God's Word that they often are wrung out like a sponge and left dry and used by the sink. Getting involved with a group gives you an opportunity to be filled and a group to support you as you carry out God's work.

Finally, the third step is to serve as a leader in a class, but remember, you do not have to be the teacher to be a leader. Some pastors may thrive as a Sunday school teacher, but for many, the chance to be a care group leader or an outreach director has given them the chance to do something they care about, but no longer get to do as much in their role as pastor. When I first began as a Sunday school teacher, I was blessed to have the pastor of our church serve as the evangelism leader of our class. As a gifted evangelist, he brought a lot of energy to our class and equipped us with many tools to share the gospel, while he was able to have at least one area of his church ministry where he could focus on doing what God had gifted him to do. Seeing him in this role elevated Sunday school at our church and encouraged several other gifted leaders to commit to serve as evangelism leaders, because they knew if it was valuable enough for the pastor to do, it was an important job.

The bottom line is simple: the best way that a leader can lead is by doing. In Ezra's case, the people understood how important studying and understanding God's Word was because they understood how Ezra valued studying and teaching God's Word. In the same way, pastors can lead their Sunday school by teaching God's Word personally, whether it is in the pulpit, in training sessions, or in groups. The best way to lead Sunday school teachers to carry out the work of the Kingdom is to bring out the Book, study it, apply it, and teach it personally.

Questions for Discussion

1. What leadership insights can you gain from Ezra's public proclamation of the Word in Nehemiah 8:1-12?
2. Are there differences in how one learns in a large group setting and a small group? If so, what are they?
3. What leadership behaviors did you glean from Ezra's commitment to teach God's Word personally?
4. Is it important for a pastor to be involved in Sunday school personally? Why or why not?

A Chance for Deeper Thought

One of the hardest parts of leading any small group ministry as a pastor is training leaders, but as we mentioned in the chapter, two key steps to help are organization and reaching out. Taking the values your Sunday school holds as a guide (or using the Four Stages of Group Development), create a quarterly training schedule for your church. This schedule should include the time and date for each meeting, the length of time of the meeting, the subject of training meeting, and a list of what resources or people will be needed to carry out this training. After you have made this schedule, write a 2 paragraph reflection on how this would be helpful and on what resources you would need to consistently plan training sessions for Sunday school.

6

GETTING STARTED

As nerdy as this may sound, one of my favorite types of televisions shows to watch are the ones that show how things are made. As a process thinker, I enjoy seeing all the steps that turn a piece of wood into a bookshelf or transform a random bean into designer chocolate. As a curious person, I like to learn why certain items are added to a design or how products turn out just right. But, for all the shows I have watched on how things are made, the truth is that I rarely have made any of those things myself. Simply knowing that oranges can be squeezed to make juice is a good starting place, but by itself, it never gives you the sweet refreshment of juice. If the goal is enjoying juice, you must start squeezing oranges; in the same way, if the goal of learning how to lead Sunday school is to guide your leaders to teach God's Word, care for one another, and take the gospel out into the world, you cannot be content to merely learn how to lead – you must get to work!

In this chapter, I want to give you two tools to help you begin putting these leadership principles we have gleaned from Ezra into place as you lead your Sunday school. Throughout this work, we have discussed the importance of expectations for leaders, so in the first section, we will consider how you can develop written expectations and guidelines for your Sunday school leaders. Then, we will look at the Pastor's Sunday School Scorecard, a tool that you can use to help you put into place the principles that we have learned throughout this work.

A Written Set of Guidelines for Sunday School Leaders

Throughout this work, we have mentioned the importance of expectations and standards for Sunday school leaders in the areas of recruiting leaders, holding leaders accountable, and as the starting point for training leaders. Having clear and well-defined expectations help Sunday school leaders understand what they are trying to accomplish and how they can succeed at their task. The practice of putting them in writing calls a pastor and church leaders to take these standards seriously, as it adds a sense of permanency to their work. Just as an archer desires a brightly painted bullseye, having a clear picture of what is expected gives Sunday school leaders a clear goal in their work, while also maintaining a standard of holiness and competency among leadership.

Yet, in creating standards for Sunday school leaders, pastors and churches must use wisdom and discretion. On one hand, if the standards set are too general or too broad, they will not give clear direction as to how leaders should conduct themselves or what they should seek to do. On the other hand, if standards are too stringent, they can quickly become pharisaical and raise a standard that is impossible to reach. One of the best ways to combat this danger is to seek counsel in the formation of these standards; a pastor should not attempt to walk this journey alone, but rather, he should enlist the help of his deacons, elders, or trusted Sunday school leaders to ensure that standards for Sunday school leaders reflect the values of the church and are reasonable and just.

After considering who should be involved in the process, the first step is to begin with standards of leadership, sometimes known as a Leadership Covenant. This document lays forth expectations to be held by all Sunday school leaders, regardless of the role they fill, and is primarily concerned with the character and lifestyle of the leader. Such a document should include a commitment to:

- Grow in my faith and personal devotion to Christ through consistent Bible study
- Faithfully support the work of the church through attendance and financial giving
- Be holy in all of life, both in things seen and not seen publicly
- Share my faith regularly with others
- Pray for my group and my church
- Be a faithful leader of my family, including in marriage and parenthood

To be a leader in Sunday school is to be an ambassador of the Kingdom of God, so the goal of this covenant is to make clear what such a representative should look like. While my list above gives a basic starting point, your church may have further standards you wish to add along the character of a Sunday school leader, but keep in mind that your aim is to present a simple picture of what a disciple of Christ who leads should look like.

The Leadership Covenant is an important starting point, both in recruiting and in calling leaders to follow God's standards. For recruiters, the Covenant gives a clear picture of the believer who is prepared to take on leadership roles in Sunday school ministry, helping them to have a baseline standard to begin from. The Covenant also serves as the basis of accountability for leaders, giving those in authority a clear standard to judge whether one is living according to God's standards. In agreeing to follow the Leadership Covenant, the leader is publicly committing to follow the ways of God and to be willing to be held accountable for them, an endeavor that should be taken seriously and honored as such. One of the most powerful times in my ministry was seeing a group of leaders pray together and publicly sign a Leadership Covenant before the church, agreeing to maintain holiness as they led the people of God.

The next step in establishing standards comes in the form of a job description for specific roles. While the Leadership Covenant serves to provide expectations for all leaders, specific job descriptions are much more detailed and are intended to lay out the tasks expected of leaders in the various positions they occupy. Each job description should include the goal of the position, the skills needed to carry it out well, and the commitment the position requires. It is important that you make clear what skills are needed for each position, because this will form the basis of how you train each position and help leaders grow.

Though there could be any number of positions you choose to recruit for in your Sunday school, churches will need to consider at least the three leadership posts common to all Sunday schools to develop job descriptions for: teacher, care leader, and outreach leader. To help you begin the discussion of necessary skills and commitments need for these roles, the chart below includes suggestions for each of the three posts; it is not exhaustive, but rather, is meant to give you a starting point in thinking about the types of skills your leaders will need and the commitments you are calling them toward.

While it can be intimidating to consider writing out standards and guidelines for Sunday school leaders, the practice will serve great benefits for a pastor as he seeks to lead Sunday school. Having a Leadership Covenant and job descriptions gives the pastor a simple structure to ensure that Sunday school leaders are aware of their call to represent Christ as leaders and ensures that they know the skills they need and can develop to do their tasks well. It also protects a pastor when he is forced to deal with messes, as the standards were known ahead of time and discipline measures are not arbitrarily given.

	Necessary Skills	Commitments
Teacher	– prepare a Bible lesson that explains the passage clearly – teach in a way that encourages participation and involvement – work with an apprentice to train future teachers and leaders – serve as a general leader of the weekly meeting	– spend adequate time during the week to study and prepare a lesson – teach each week or secure a substitute who can fill in for you – invest in an apprentice by studying with them, giving them parts of the lesson to teach, and helping them understand the task
Care Leader	– determining needs for care ministry in the group – welcoming newcomers to the group and connecting them to members who can pray with them and support them – delegate care ministries to care group leaders to ensure members are cared for	– contacting those who were absent from the group – compiling a prayer list for the group and making it available – leading the group to celebrate important dates (birthdays, anniversaries, etc.) of members – coordinating care ministries for the needs of the class

Outreach Leader	– share faith personally and teach group members how to share the gospel – plan events that will involve group members in going out and sharing the gospel – leading the class in praying for the lost and getting involved in mission opportunities	– present testimonies of group members sharing their faith each month – encourage members to share the gospel monthly by teaching ways to do so – planning quarterly events for the class to get involved in missions and evangelism

For many churches, this will be a new concept, so you must use wisdom in implementing these written standards. When we began the process of implementing standards at one of the churches I served, we used a phase-in approach to acclimate our leaders to the new standards. In the first year, we explained and taught our standards in training times and used them as a guide in recruiting leaders. In the second year, we asked leaders to commit to our Leadership Covenant and to work with us to ensure that the skills and commitments listed in our job descriptions were both reasonable and necessary. By the third year, our leaders publicly signed the Leadership Covenant and committed to following the job descriptions annually.

In describing this process, though, there is one word of caution to offer. Change is sometimes very difficult and in implementing standards for your Sunday school leaders, you will be creating change. It may take some time to convince your church and your Sunday school leaders of the value of holding your leaders to standards and to create buy-in for the leaders. Although we would like hope this would not be the case, you will most likely lose some leaders when you begin to raise the bar of expectations. However, the fruit of your work will become evident when Sunday school leaders take seriously the call to teach God's word, care for His people, and share the gospel as ambassadors of Christ; weather the storm and you will see the blessing of your work!

The Pastor's Sunday School Scorecard

When I graduated high school, my cousin and I took a weeklong trip with the goal of trying as many iconic foods and seeing as many sports halls of fame as we could. It was a great and memorable trip, but after covering so much distance and so many different histories and tastes, it was difficult to get a good grasp of what we had seen. In a trip that spanned several days and hundreds of miles, it was hard to remember specific lessons learned from a single day or a span of miles. In many ways, that is the same feeling that comes to mind with this book, as we have covered a lot of ground in our examination of how pastors can lead Sunday school; how can we put into place the lessons we have learned?

To this end, I would like to present you with the Pastor's Sunday School Scorecard, a tool intended to help you apply the leadership lessons we have gleaned from Ezra's example as you lead Sunday school. This chart contains five major leadership areas measured in three progressive steps of involvement. Each behavior includes a 1-3 scale to help you determine your participation level, where 1 indicates "do not participate at all," 2 indicates "sometimes participate," and 3 indicates "regularly participate."

The Scorecard summarizes the principles we have covered into five major areas that pastors can lead in. In Recruiting, we are considering how pastors are involved in seeking prospects for new leaders and working with a team of recruiters to identify and train leaders. Training and Creating Standards are placed to together to measure how a pastor is engaged in creating and communicating the standards Sunday school leaders are called to follow. As a pastor carries weight in a variety of settings in the church, there are two categories related to the pastor's promotion of Sunday school, one concerned with his promotion from the platform and the other concerned with his promotion at the class level. Finally, the last leadership area looks at how the pastor is involved in helping Sunday school leaders teach God's word.

The three progressive steps explain how a pastor may increase his involvement level in each major leadership area as he leads Sunday school. Step one is the starting point for each area, as it offers a first step to leading in the given area. In step two, the pastor is beginning to dig into the work of leading Sunday school, as these behaviors present an added involvement beyond step one. Finally, step three constitutes behaviors pastors may use when they are taking the lead in Sunday school; these behaviors require significant involvement that often necessitate weekly investments.

As you look over the Scorecard, evaluate where you are in your leadership of these five areas and consider which steps you can take to grow as a leader. It can be helpful to make note of your total score from time to time to determine if you are more involved or less involved in these leadership behaviors over time.

The Pastor's Sunday School Scorecard			
Leadership Area	Step One Getting Started	Step Two Digging In	Step Three Taking the Lead
Recruiting	Ask church leaders and current Sunday school leaders for recommendations for future leaders	Prepare a job description for potential leaders and train recruiters in it	Train current leaders to identify and train leaders within their classes
	1 2 3	1 2 3	1 2 3
Training and Creating Standards	Write out your Sunday school values and expectations and teach these standards to your leaders	Provide training opportunities that align with your Sunday school values and job descriptions	Call upon your Sunday school leaders to commit to your Leadership Covenant and job descriptions
	1 2 3	1 2 3	1 2 3
Promotion from the Platform	Talk about Sunday school groups, meeting times, locations, and events from the pulpit	Reference material from Sunday school (verses, stories) in sermon illustrations	Recognize Sunday school leaders and events specifically in the service
	1 2 3	1 2 3	1 2 3
Promotion in the Rooms	Greet people and Sunday school leaders as they come to their groups. Check in with leaders in passing on a regular basis	Go to a group on a regular basis!	Serve as a leader in a Sunday school group (You don't have to be the teacher!)
	1 2 3	1 2 3	1 2 3
Teaching	Model good Bible study practices and teaching in your preaching ministry	Provide resources to Sunday school leaders covering Bible study methods and teaching practices	Lead or coordinate a Bible study methods and teaching techniques class for your leaders
	1 2 3	1 2 3	1 2 3

Remember that change takes time and do not let this serve as a discouraging tool to show where you lack, but rather, use it as a guide as you follow the Lord in leading His people. The goal is not merely to reach step three on this Scorecard, but rather, the goal is to help you as you seek to follow the model of Ezra, who set his heart to study the Law of the Lord, and to do it, and to teach His statutes and rules. Set your heart and get to work!

Questions for Discussion

1. Why is it important to have written standards for Sunday school leaders?
2. What kind of traits do you think should be included in a Leadership Covenant?
3. How would it help a pastor to have job descriptions for Sunday school leaders?
4. What are some ways you could introduce and incorporate standards for Sunday school leaders?

A Chance for Deeper Thought

In this chapter, we introduced the Pastor's Sunday School Scorecard to give you a practical guide to leading Sunday school as a pastor. Using the Scorecard as a guide, reflect on your leadership of Sunday school and determine what areas you would like to work on in your leadership. In a 2-3 page paper, explain which area you would like to develop in your leadership, including the reason why you chose that area, and create a plan to guide you in that development. Your plan should include action steps and time markers to help you carry out your plan.

7
FINAL THOUGHTS

Combing through the literature for this project, I came across a quote that seems like a good place to end our journey. Noting how pastors are trained extensively in Bible study, theology, and preaching, but rarely prepared to lead Sunday school, the researcher continued:

> To further compound the issue, much of the literature on the mechanics and methods of Sunday school is either directed toward lay leaders and education directors or written about the organization and techniques of Sunday school for large churches. For the average pastor, this is akin to turning off the lights and asking him to grab the red can from the closet; he is searching for resources in a field he does not know and has little guidance to point him in the right direction... [This study] is a call to encourage writers and publishers to produce resources designed to teach pastors how to be involved and how to lead Sunday school to guide their congregations to follow God together. (Smith, 2014, p.199)

The convicting part for me as a writer is that this was my quote four years ago! Yet, though it took some time to produce, this work is a response to that call. My hope is that you will find these thoughts and tips to be helpful as you begin to lead Sunday school in your church.

The study of Ezra's work provided a rewarding investigation of the role a leader committed to studying, doing, and teaching God's word can have on a group of people. Though Ezra held a prominent place in the history of the Jews, with many referring to him as the "second Moses," discussions of the scribe are conspicuously absent in many of the contemporary conversations on biblical leadership, as his contemporary, Nehemiah, often takes center stage. Yet, in exploring the leadership behaviors of Ezra, we can see a leader that modern day pastors can relate to, as he was an expositor with a heart for God that extended into a love for His people; he is never seen charging ahead alone, nor is he seen presenting an expansive vision for the people, though, as Nehemiah's life exhibits, there is a place for such things in leadership. On the other hand, the temptation to say that he was a scholar living in the shadows would also be a mischaracterization; he was a teacher of God's people and the three vignettes of his life shown in Scripture revealed a man who was constantly in the middle of things, proclaiming God's Law, teaching others how to apply it, and being ready to respond quickly and decisively when God's hand is at work in the life of the people, be it through the urgings of a pagan king, the confessions of a sinful nation, or the call to teach and explain God's ways publicly and in groups.

Ezra's leadership behaviors revealed a model based around three central themes: recruiting and training leaders, calling leaders to be accountable to God's standards, and personally teaching the Bible. These leadership behaviors produced leaders who were capable of leading others in a study of God's word in groups and, in so doing, a returning band of exiles were transformed into a people who worshipped God according to God's law for the first time in centuries. Pastors, these same behaviors can serve as your guide as you lead Sunday school at your church (a summary chart of all these behaviors may be found in the Appendix).

Yet, I fear that some pastors may walk away from this book discouraged by the prospect of leading Sunday school. After all, the task will require changes and time for most pastors, an investment that some are not willing or able to give. But I want to encourage you to set your heart anew to the work of the Lord and do the best you can do. Sunday school can serve as a powerful tool for the pastor as he leads his church, mobilizing the church to teach God's Word, care for one another, and share the gospel in a way that a pastor simply cannot do on his own. There is always a cost in obtaining anything of value and while you may have to endure some struggles initially as you invest in Sunday school, the fruit of your efforts will shine brilliantly in the disciples who boldly teach, care, and go for the sake of Christ's Kingdom. Vieth's (1957) postscript captures this reality well:

> We may have given the impression that the life of the church school leader consists only of problems and heartaches, of thorns and never a rose. This is not the case. It also has its glory and joy. The glory is that of working in the most important undertaking of the church, of serving him whom we call Master. The joy is that of working with a selected group of God's people in the church school staff, and with them, seeing generations of young people growing up in discipleship to that same Master. (p.265)

Set your hearts, friend, to study the Law of the Lord, and to do it, and to teach his statutes and rules to all around you; it is a commitment you will never regret.

APPENDIX
Ezra's Leadership Behaviors
And Corresponding Behaviors For Pastors

Ezra's Leadership Behaviors	Leadership Behaviors for Senior Pastors
Recruiting and Training Leaders	
Pray for future leaders	– Pray for potential Sunday school leaders
Select and train a group of recruiters	– Choose Sunday school leaders as recruiters – Direct recruiters to potential leaders – Use spiritual gift inventories or interest surveys to find potential leaders – Stay involved and aware of the recruiting process.
Recruit specific roles with clear expectations	– Define specific roles of leadership in Sunday school – Lay out clear (written) guidelines that leaders can commit to and understand – Hold and attend regular training sessions – Offer resources to leaders for personal development – Provide leaders with training in Christian doctrine and discipleship

Holding Leaders to God's Standards	
Teach God's standards for living	– Faithfully teach and preach God's Word – Make the standards of Christian living clear to leaders through covenants and training opportunities
Respond to sin with a call for confession and repentance	– Encourage fallen leaders to pursue repentance and obedience to God
Work with leaders to fairly adjudicate cases of sin and broken standards	– Select a group of mature Sunday school leaders to develop clear standards and disciplinary measures – Select a group who can serve as an accountability team to investigate allegations and execute disciplinary actions
Teaching God's Word Personally	
Proclaim God's Word publicly to all people	– Faithfully teach and preach God's Word – Utilize expository preaching principles
Encourage leaders to explain and apply God's Word in small groups.	– Use the pulpit and the influence of the pastor to encourage Sunday school leaders and involvement in Sunday school – Serve as a champion and cheerleader of Sunday school
Teach the Scriptures in small groups	– Take part in a Sunday school class and small groups – Lead a Sunday school class

REFERENCES

Allen, L.C. (2003). Ezra & Nehemiah. In Allen, L. C., & Laniak, T. S., *Ezra, Nehemiah, Esther: Based on the New International Version* (pp.3-159). Peabody, Mass: Hendrickson Publishers.

Blanchard, K. & Hodges, P. (2005). *Lead like Jesus: Lessons from the greatest leadership role model of all times.* Nashville, TN: W Publishing Group.

Breneman, M. (1993). *Ezra, Nehemiah, Esther.* Nashville, TN: Broadman & Holman Publishers.

Fensham, F. C. (1991). *The books of Ezra and Nehemiah.* Grand Rapids, MI: Eerdmans.

Francis, D. (2011). *Missionary Sunday school: One mission. His story. Every person.* Nashville, TN: LifeWay Press.

Francis, D., & Braddy, K. (2013). *3 Roles for guiding groups: Teacher, shepherd leader.* Nashville, TN: LifeWay Press.

Hemphill, K. (1996). *Revitalizing the Sunday morning dinosaur: A Sunday school growth strategy for the 21st century.* Nashville, TN: Broadman & Holman Publishers.

Hemphill. K, & Taylor, B. (2001). *Ten best practices to make your Sunday school work.* Nashville, TN: LifeWay Church Resources.

Hunt, J. (1997). *You can double your class in two years or less.* Loveland, CO: Group.

Kidner, D. (1979). *Ezra and Nehemiah: An introduction and commentary.* Downers Grove, IL: Inter-Varsity Press.

Keil, C. F., & Delitzsch, F. (1996). *Ezra, Nehemiah, Esther & the book of Job.* Peabody, MA: Hendrickson Publishers.

McCready, W.O. (1986). Priests and levites. In *The International Standard Bible Encyclopedia.* (Vol. 3, pp. 966-970). Grand Rapids, MI: William B. Eerdmans Publishing Company.

Mims, G. (2003). *The kingdom focused church: A compelling image of an achievable future for your church.* Nashville, TN: Broadman & Holman Publishers.

Myers, J. M. (1965). *Ezra, Nehemiah.* Garden City, NJ: Doubleday.

Parr, S.R. (2002). Key #5 – Leaders are trained for effectiveness. In S. Parr (Ed.), *Key strategies for a healthy Sunday school (pp. 28-36).* Atlanta, GA: Bible Study Ministries.

Parr, S.R. (2010). *Sunday school that really works: A strategy for connecting congregations and communities.* Grand Rapids, MI: Kregel.

Parr, S.R. (2013). The state of Sunday school today. In S.R. Parr (Ed.), *Sunday school that really excels* (pp.23-35). Grand Rapids, MI: Kregel.

Pritchett, B. (2013). Excels in revitalizing an established ministry. In S.R. Parr (Ed.), *Sunday school that really excels* (pp. 59-68). Grand Rapids, MI: Kregel.

Rainer, T. S. (1999). *High expectations: The remarkable secret for keeping people in your church.* Nashville, TN: Broadman & Holman Publishers.

Smith, J.A. (2014). *Following the ways of Ezra: an exploratory study of the relationship* between a senior pastor's involvement in leading Sunday school and church health (Unpublished doctoral dissertation). Southeastern Baptist Theological Seminary, Wake Forest, NC.

Stetzer, E., & Dodson, M. (2007). *Comeback churches: How 300 churches turned around and yours can too.* Nashville, Tenn.: B & H Publishing Group.

Stetzer, E., & Rainer, T. (2010). *Transformational church: Creating a new scorecard for congregations*. Nashville, Tenn.: B & H Publishing Group.

Taylor, A. (2003). *The six core values of Sunday school: A philosophical, practical, & passionate approach to Sunday school*. Canton, GA: Riverstone Group.

Taylor, A. (2009). *Sunday school in HD: Sharpening the focus on what makes your church healthy*. Nashville, TN: B&H Publishing Group.

Vieth, P. H. (1957). *The church school: the organization, administration, and supervision of Christian education in the local church*. Philadelphia, Pa: Christian Education Press.

Williamson, H. G. M. (1985). *Ezra, Nehemiah*. Waco, Tex: Word Books.

Yamauchi, E (1988). Ezra – Nehemiah. In F.E. Gaebelein (Ed.), *The expositor's Bible commentary* (Vol. 4, pp 565-774). Grand Rapids, MI: Zondervan.

ABOUT THE AUTHOR

Justin Smith is the proud father of Nate, Joanna, and Sam. He received the Master of Divinity in Biblical Studies from Southern Evangelical Seminary in Matthews, NC and the Doctor of Education from Southeastern Baptist Theological Seminary in Wake Forest, NC. With experience in serving a wide variety of ministries, as well as training many pastors and ministry leaders, Justin loves to work with churches and leaders as they develop the gifts God has given them and use them for His glory, both in His church and around the world.

www.ingramcontent.com/pod-product-compliance
Lightning Source LLC
Chambersburg PA
CBHW070817050426
42452CB00011B/2081